CRYSTAL CRUISES

THE CRYSTAL CRUISES COOKBOOK

Recipes inspired by the world in which we sail...

Crystal Cruises

2049 Century Park East, Suite 1400

Los Angeles, California 90067

Cuisine is made by people, with their hands and their hearts. As our chefs travel the world they have the good fortune to discover a wealth of culinary treasures. Wandering local markets, visiting farms and vineyards, they smell the local smells, taste the local flavors, experience the varied moods of the land. Sitting around a table and enjoying conversation and a meal, they feel the energy and vitality of the people.

In this setting, food is more than simple sustenance. It becomes the essence of the people themselves: their imagination, passion, and care, their intimate bond with nature and one another. Over the centuries each culture and landscape has evolved its own unique flavors, which travel with the tide of events and the movement of people to distant lands. Our chefs wish to dedicate this book to the people of the world, who have inspired them to bring the culinary traditions of countless nations to the tables of Crystal Cruises.

The laughter, the day's shared events, the surprises, and the love — all create an experience that nourishes both the body and the soul. So we would also like to dedicate this book to the tireless efforts of our culinary team, whose goal is to bring the warmth of their hearths and homes to your table. It is their devotion which ensures that as you sail the seven seas with us, you will agree…it is a wonderful world.

∼ TABLE OF CONTENTS ∼

In all the years that I have sailed with Crystal Cruises, as a Guest Chef or simply as a guest, I've heard countless guests wish they could take home the great recipes they enjoy on board. Not surprising, with the range of superb dishes that Toni Neumeister and his team of chefs provide. Now, Toni and his chefs have satisfied their guests' wishes with "The Crystal Cruises Cookbook," a highly personal collection of some of their most prized dishes. A culinary classic is born.

As they cruise around the world, the chef-artists of Crystal Cruises have access to the best recipes and ingredients in the world — no kitchen anywhere on earth has this great advantage, which constantly raises them to new creative heights.

With their European touch, techniques, and precision, they are able to serve almost a thousand guests non-stop with world-class cuisine. It is a joy to watch them at work. The kitchen is orchestrated like the finest ballet. But even with these techniques and fine organization, the cuisine would not be complete without the natural and freshest ingredients they find in each port of call, and over all without their love of cooking and pleasing the guests.

Their latest tour de force has been to translate the techniques and secrets that are performed by a large team of highly trained skilled chefs in the vast galleys into recipes that can be easily executed in your home kitchen. And, what a pleasure to have each recipe matched with appropriate wines. It shows the depth of the magnificent, well-balanced wine list and cellar on board.

The next best thing to dining aboard Crystal Cruises is owning a copy of this book, an entire world of great and intensely flavored recipes. You now have a road map that points the way to great eating and fine living. Merci, Toni, for showing us, even when we're back on land, that we still live between the sea and paradise.

André Soltner

$\mathcal{F}$ine cuisine is a vital part of what we do, and a source of special pride.

Step into the bright, airy spaces of our ships and enter the leisurely, eternal rhythms of life at sea. This is the setting for a unique culinary journey, together with the master chefs of Crystal Cruises.

Over time, our commitment to excellence has earned the highest awards from gourmet critics, and the consistent praise of our guests. Our Culinary Director Toni Neumeister and key members of his team recently presented a dinner at New York's renowned James Beard House, the Carnegie Hall of cooking. This is a distinction only the top chefs on earth can claim, and the first time James Beard House has ever recognized the chef of a cruise line. *The Crystal Wine & Food Festival* is widely acclaimed in cruising. Each year a celebrity cast of Guest Chefs and wine experts join our ships from around the world, to share their culinary secrets with our guests. Distinguished chefs like André Soltner, Barbara Tropp, Jacques Pépin, Wolfgang Puck, and Charles Dale regularly take part, and each has honored us by contributing a recipe to this book — showing their respect for our culinary standards.

We've achieved these results because we believe that cooking is one of life's special pleasures, a living expression of the cultures and landscapes through which we travel. In each distant port, our chefs find an exotic ingredient, a celebrated local dish, a regional cooking style that sparks their imagination. Sometimes the mood of the region itself inspires them: the feel of the land, the spirit of the people. The essence of each region infuses our cuisine — and each of the recipes you are about to enjoy.

But to be a true artist, you must first be a skilled craftsman. Our chefs are masters of the three fundamentals of fine cuisine: materials, preparation, and presentation. They work only with the finest and freshest ingredients, garnered from around the world. To bring out the sublime flavors of these materials, they use the time-honored skills and culinary knowledge of France, home to one of the world's noblest gourmet traditions.

And as in all truly distinguished cuisine, their creations delight not only the palate, but the senses and the imagination as well. This command of cooking fundamentals underlies their regionally inspired artistry, giving their recipes a controlled polish and international perspective that is unique.

When you are in the middle of the ocean,

assembling all the pieces of the elaborate puzzle

that is the perfect gourmet meal

takes remarkable teamwork.

A great recipe begins with great ingredients, the pure, true tastes of the sea and the earth. So as we sail the globe, we are careful to select only the finest and freshest ingredients in every port: fragrant Brazilian mangoes, earthy asparagus from fertile Alpine valleys and truffles from the cool forests, sweet Dungeness crab from Alaska and tender, pink-fleshed Opah from warm tropical waters. Ensuring that supplies meet our high standards isn't easy. Our Purchasing Department, together with the Culinary Director and his staff, closely monitors a vast network of international suppliers. They visit markets and meet with buyers, ensuring that our high standards for quality are maintained no matter where we are in the world. And beyond quality and freshness, the ingredients must be right—precisely the right raw materials for each dish we prepare. When a specific ingredient is not available locally, we fly it in. We will airlift live Maine lobsters to Tauranga or fresh California berries to Dakar, making sure the precious supplies are waiting pierside when the ship docks. A complicated task, but the results speak for themselves. With this fresh bounty of nature, our chefs infuse each dish with distinctive textures, intense aromas, and flavors of remarkable purity.

To enable each delicious ingredient of a dish to speak for itself, our chefs use the secrets and skills of French *grande cuisine*. For the last five hundred years, gourmet cooking has received more care and creative attention in France than anywhere else on earth. In the royal courts and later in great French restaurants, through generation after generation of practice, curiosity, and refinement, cuisine has gradually been raised to a high art. The French basics leave nothing to chance: there is a "right way" to chop an onion or whip egg whites into a cloudlike méringue. This treasury of methods and wisdom is the basis of our repertoire. Our chefs have spent long years of training at some of the most celebrated culinary academies and restaurants in Europe, mastering the difficult craft of fine French cooking. Decades of experience have taught them how to distill the essence of a fish or a fowl into a rich, slow-cooked stock, and how to use delicate sauces to enhance, rather than conceal, the central flavors of a dish. The time-honored techniques of French *grande cuisine* are a firm foundation for our chefs' culinary creativity. Their precision, polish, and drama infuse our cuisine, and the recipes we selected for this book.

Classical Basics

A Feast for the Senses

$\mathcal{A}$ fine dish brings complete sensory fulfillment, in a procession of colors and textures, aromas and tastes. It all starts with perfect presentation: as complex as our stately White Chocolate Cheese Tart Moderne with its dramatically sculpted chocolate and radiant red raspberries, or as simple as the casual elegance of the pale pink Broiled Salmon surrounded by the soft creamy colors of spinach and butter sauce. Each is an enticement, setting the stage for the pleasures and satisfactions to come. As the nose begins to gather a lush bouquet of up to 2,000 aromas, the tastebuds start to explore every flavor and texture within each dish. Imagine the delicately sweet crabmeat, aromatic tarragon, and robust Brie of Alaskan Crab Soup; the woody Porcini mushrooms and mellow, meaty Bolognese sauce melding in our slow-cooked Prego Lasagne; or the lush chocolate warmth and cool Cognac cream of the Warm Chocolate-Hazelnut Pudding — each distinctive fragrance and sumptuous taste in perfect harmony. At the end of this stirring experience, you discover that fine cuisine brings satisfaction for the spirit as well as the body. Yet one last sensory level remains, which transcends the familiar five senses and enters a broader, more instinctive realm. Gentle music, friendly conversation, the warmth and decorum of the Maître d' and his team of waiters, windows overlooking an infinite, wave-washed horizon — every detail matters, and all are a part of this crucial, elusive quality. Only when each subtle element is in place, and each sense is fully satisfied, can the magic of a great meal take place.

$\mathscr{O}$ur chefs, dining staff, provisions and stores specialists,

and countless other experts work together with perfect precision,

becoming one vast team.

It is a remarkable performance

that continues around the clock.

5:00am *The waves are cloaked in darkness, our guests are still fast asleep. Yet not far away, a team of ten chefs, cooks, and assistant cooks is hard at work. Some are cooking breakfast at the ovens and griddles, others review menus and inspect the day's store of food for freshness. In the Bakery nearby, four bakers are wreathed in the heavenly aromas of over twenty different kinds of pastries, croissants, muffins, and fresh breads, while two coffee brewers are preparing to make fresh-ground coffee, espresso, and cappuccino in the Coffee*

Pantry. **6:00am** *As the sun rises slowly from the glistening waters, waiters and their assistants collect starched uniforms and fresh linens from the Laundry, then report to their respective restaurants and begin breakfast prep. In the Garde-Manger fourteen people are slicing tropical fruits, smoked salmon, and other chilled breakfast items. Much of their handiwork goes to the Lido Buffet, where the first guests are beginning to arrive. They are greeted by a tantalizing buffet of cheeses, hams and salami, pastries, bagels, eggs, berries, cold and hot cereals, even miso soup, as well as made-to-order omelettes and Belgian waffles, all scrupulously overseen by the Executive Chef.* **7:00am** *As most guests are just starting to savor their breakfast, specialists throughout the ship are already planning lunch and dinner. The Executive Chef begins orchestrating the day's menus with his Chefs de Cuisine. Six chefs in the Soup Kitchen are slicing vegetables and making soups from scratch. The butcher and his assistants prepare select meats in the Butcher Shop, while in the Fish*

Kitchen, four poissonniers are choosing and filleting fresh fish and seafood. In the Pastry Shop, under the direction of the Executive Pastry Chef, seven confectioners begin making pies and creams, each day baking 100 cakes and 1,000 basic pastry items, such as hand-made truffles and Tea Time sweets and savories, as well as a range of specialty cookies. By now the Main Galley is in full swing, with chefs preparing roasts and making fresh pasta by hand,

sauciers stirring up rich sauces and stocks. **8:00am** *Out on the bustling pier, the Ships Stores Manager and Executive Chef are checking each crate and basket of the abundant fresh ingredients that a day in port brings—up to sixty tons of supplies at the beginning of a cruise. Every item is stored safely away in the ship's temperature-controlled provision holds. At this time the Chefs de Cuisine of the Specialty Restaurants set to work on the evening meal. There are ducks to marinate and air dry, stocks and rices to prepare, special sauces to begin simmering.* **9:00am** *As*

guests emerge for an after-breakfast stroll on the Promenade Deck, new venues are continually coming online. The Executive Chef meets with the Food & Beverage Manager and department heads to ensure perfect coordination between kitchen and waiters and bar staff for all events of the day. After collecting an assortment of breakfast specialties from the Main Galley, the Bistro Team lays out a convivial breakfast service. Meanwhile, out in the balmy sea breezes, the staff of the Trident Grill begins baking pizzas and preparing special wrap sandwiches, burgers, and other lunch favorites, served all afternoon long. **10:00am** *As one meal ends, arrangements for the next begin. With breakfast service coming to a close, a team of silver polishers sets to work in a special area of the Main Galley, buffing the silver service to a high sheen. Nearby, a squad of fifteen has begun washing breakfast dishes, in two Dishwashing Zones that will be active all day long. Preparations for lunch and dinner continue in the Garde-Manger, where a dozen*

experts are making salads, terrines, and patés, carving radishes into roses, melons into graceful swans. Around now the Executive Chef finds a moment to sit down in his office, in order to plan menus for the next few days and organize provisions accordingly. **11:00am** *In the Crystal Dining Room, assistant waiters begin folding napkins, setting tables with fresh flowers and sparkling stemware, in preparation for the lunch service. The Cellar Master and the Executive Chef meet to select the wines best suited for lunch and dinner. Meanwhile the Bistro Team is arranging a tempting selection of afternoon snacks, including cheeses, olives, cured meats, and pastries.* **12:00 noon** *As the sun reaches its zenith, lunch begins in the Crystal Dining Room, the Lido Café, the Trident Grill, and the Bistro. During Themed Buffets the Lido Deck is transformed into another realm, with stylish decorations and an enticing selection of regional foods, including Asia Café with delicacies from across the Orient,*

and Cuisine of the Sun with its sun-blessed Mediterranean specialities. **1:00pm** *While guest meals are obviously the focus of our attention, there is the little matter of over 500 crew members to be fed. The Sous Chef and four assistants are hard at work in the Crew Galley, where they have been preparing crew meals since 5:30am, in a variety of ethnic styles to satisfy all 32 nationalities of our crew.* **2:00pm** *Work continues throughout the ship, building towards Tea Time, dinner, and beyond. In the Bakery and the Pastry Shop, the Coffee Pantry and the Garde-Manger, the Soup Kitchen, the Vegetable Station, the Fish Kitchen, and the Butcher Shop, people carry out their specialized tasks all day long.* **3:00pm** *By now assistant waiters and staff are collecting a range of sweets and savories for Tea Time. Soon the Palm Court hosts one of several distinctive events, including Mozart Tea with staff dressed in the brocade and lace*

costumes of Old Vienna, serving a sinfully rich selection of Austrian cakes and pastries; and the aristocratic style of English Colonial Tea, complete with scones, clotted cream, and assorted sweets. Meanwhile, guests linger poolside at the Trident Ice Cream Bar all afternoon, choosing from an array of ice creams, frozen yogurts, toppings, and cookies. **4:00pm** *With lunch and Tea Time over, the staff turns its full attention to dinner, the culmination of each culinary day. Already chefs in the Specialty Restaurants are cooking soups from stocks prepared that morning, organizing garnishes, and marinating fish in olive oil and herbs. They also begin elaborate main dishes like Prego's famous Lasagne, which takes over two hours to prepare, and must compose itself for two hours more before the final baking. Others begin making hors d'oeuvres for cocktail hour. The Pastry Team resumes work, putting final touches on their dinner masterpieces for all restaurants.* **5:00pm** *The evening shift of bread bakers starts work, and waiters*

report for duty at their respective restaurants. Each Specialty Restaurants has an Assistant Cellar Master, five waiters, one headwaiter, and one Maître d'; while the Crystal Dining Room has no less than sixty waiters, together with five headwaiters, a Maître d', a Cellar Master, and his team of six sommeliers. The Maître d' briefs his team of waiters, reviewing each speciality item on the menu and coaching them on proper serving technique; the Cellar Master meets

with his sommeliers to discuss the evening's menu, and the characteristics of the wines they will be recommending. By **6:00pm**, as the sunset's golden light spreads across the waves, the first dinner guests enter the Specialty Restaurants; soon Main Seating begins in the Crystal Dining Room. The Maître d' greets his guests by name, the headwaiter escorts them to their favorite table. Before long all galleys are a flurry of activity; the Main Galley is working at what staff and crew call "Full Power," with the Executive Chef at the helm. Delicacies arrive from around the ship, chefs put the finishing touches on their dinner creations, arranging silver trays and china plates under

the watchful eye of the Executive Chef. **7:00pm** Main Seating in the Crystal Dining Room is at its height. Waiters glide in and out of the gleaming galley doors, passing from the clatter and clouds of steam of the kitchen to the soft lighting and gentle conversation among the guests. Sommeliers visit each table, exchanging wine ideas and a friendly word with the guests, helping them find the vintage that best fits their meal and personal tastes. Dinner is also being served in the Crew Galley, where the galley staff prepares the evening meal for the entire crew. **8:00pm** Sunlight has faded to dusk in the panoramic windows of the Crystal Dining Room. In the brief time between Main and Late Seatings, waiters move swiftly around the silent dining room, spreading crisp white linens, setting tables with new crystal, silver, china, and brilliant flowers. Soon guests begin to arrive once more, and the drama begins anew.

The Executive Chef takes a moment to ensure that work is proceeding smoothly in the Prego, Kyoto, and Jade Garden Galleys. **9:00pm** As the moon rises into the dark sky, the flurry of activity continues, and experts carry on their specialized duties at stations throughout the ship. In the Main Galley, people are still working full-speed ahead. By **10:00pm** dinner has begun to wind down, and the late-night chefs soon come on duty in the Main Galley. They prepare an elaborate assortment of midnight snacks, and remain at their stations through the night for 24-hour room service. Waiters spruce the tables once more, readying the Crystal Dining Room for tomorrow's breakfast, only hours away. **11:00pm** Before long the Dining Room is immaculately arrayed once more. Waiters who haven't yet eaten dinner head down to the Crew Cantina, where food service is available around the clock. Here they sit and talk over the day's events, wind down, refresh and refuel, then head off to sleep. **12:00 midnight** Guests who've caught a late show, been out dancing, listening to music or lingering with friends over a Cognac can now enjoy a snack in one of the elegant lounge or bar areas, perhaps an empanada or some turnovers, or a slice of smoked salmon pizza with caviar. In the Main Galley, the 28-man Cleanup Corps is washing dinner dishes, scrubbing oversized pots and braising pans, and scouring ovens, stoves, and floors, until everything is spotless and sparkling again. It's a huge task,

and they have to work fast. As they turn off the faucets and put away their buckets and sponges, the clock strikes **5:00am**, when the team of ten chefs, cooks, and assistant cooks returns to begin breakfast once more. The long day is over at last, a new day has already begun, and the 24-hour wheel of organization keeps turning!

We travel and create our cuisine as recipes have always traveled through history, moving with the ocean currents, constantly meeting new people and interacting with foreign cultures, then adding a culture and a global vision all our own. The result is a repertoire of which we are both proud and passionate.

The Crystal Cruises Cookbook commemorates the culinary experience aboard our ships.

This collection explains some of our most celebrated recipes, carefully tailored to the needs of the home chef. Throughout we will provide instructions on classic preparation and presentation, which can make the difference between a good recipe and a great one. For the wine enthusiast, we have selected wines from around the world, just as we do on board, providing complements and contrasts that can enhance the flavors of each dish. Some are from the same region as the dish and match its style; others come from across the globe, enhancing it in unexpected ways.

We have also tried to capture some of the ambience in which these dishes are enjoyed aboard our ships. Each recipe is accompanied by a headnote that explores its distinctive flavors and origins, providing a memento of the regional experience as a whole. Dishes were photographed on board to capture the warm, rich light and unforgettable moods found only at sea. In this way, cooking the Stir-Fried Opakapaka may bring back the soft tradewinds and white beaches of the boundless Pacific, the Gaucho-Style Grilled Steak may evoke some of the emotion of your first voyage along the rugged Patagonian coast. Photographs also capture the unique atmosphere of our dining venues: the Mediterranean color and regional flavors of Italy in Prego, the timeless Japanese grace of Kyoto, the exotic Asian culinary trends in Jade Garden, the Crystal Dining Room's classic elegance.

Following Crystal Harmony and Crystal Symphony as they sail the globe, *The Crystal Cruises Cookbook* showcases the recipes we serve in five regions of the world. Here you will taste the luscious ingredients and the distinctive character of each locale, as interpreted by our master chefs. By evoking in words and images the culinary experience aboard our ships, we would like to rekindle some of the great meals, friendships, and memories of cruises past, and help you embark on countless new culinary journeys of your own.

Bon voyage...
                    and bon appétit!

Classics in Nature Europe is a landscape of pure, powerful nature. Mountains rise jagged and snowcapped to the sky, the sea sculpts coastlines of cliff and fjord, in the forests a cool twilight reigns. Nature here is mighty, but endlessly generous, bringing forth a profusion of fresh, pure gifts for the table. In mountain forests bright berries grow, truffles and mushrooms sprout in fragrant shade; wild deer glide among the trees. Fish and shellfish flourish in the icy waters, while the soil nurtures flavorful vegetables — asparagus, spinach, and the ever-popular potato. Rich creams and cheeses are the farmer's pride, lush pastures nourish choice veal and pork. This natural bounty is celebrated in the kitchens of every farmstead and mountain village. Local dishes enhance the pure, genuine flavors of the ingredients with delicate sauces and simple preparations. Our executive chefs are masters of this art of culinary understatement. Most were born and raised here, and they prepare each classic dish with special pride, sharing with our guests the treasures and traditions of their homeland.

"Here Nature provides all the flavor you need.
Fish from the sea, mushrooms and berries from the forests, elk and
reindeer from the mountains, all pure and clean."

—Toni Neumeister

Bouchot mussels grow to flavorful perfection in deep-water cultivation beds on Europe's Atlantic seacoast, developing tastes and textures celebrated by seafood connoisseurs the world over. Their flesh is sweet, pale, and deliciously tender. Our simple, classic recipe exalts them with crisp white wine, light herbs, and a dollop of cream, bringing out the genuine flavors of the sea.

 The best pairing for a dish that shows both a mineral quality and a creamy herbal note is a dry, somewhat lean white wine. The crisp, appley "Sèvre et Maine Sur Lie" **Muscadet** from Chéreau-Carré of the Loire Valley, France, is a perfect accompaniment. Or, we suggest the J. Rochioli **Sauvignon Blanc** from the Russian River in California to highlight the light herbal element in the dish with its grassy, crisp profile. For a wonderful alternative, try the fruitier, citrus-noted Granbazan **Albariño** from Spain's Rias Baixas region.

in White Wine Fumet

2 tablespoons unsalted butter or
extra-virgin olive oil

6 shallots, minced

1 teaspoon white peppercorns, crushed

4 garlic cloves, minced

1 celery stalk, peeled and finely diced

1 large bunch flat-leaf (Italian)
parsley, stemmed and minced
(about ½ cup)

1 bay leaf

2 fresh thyme sprigs

2 cups dry white wine

4 pounds Bouchot mussels, scrubbed
and debearded

½ cup heavy cream

Serves 4

CHEF'S NOTES This recipe can be served as an appetizer or as a main course. Black mussels may be substituted for the Bouchot mussels.

PREPARATION In a stockpot, melt the butter or olive oil over medium heat and sauté the shallots and peppercorns for 2 minutes. Add the garlic and celery and sauté for about 1 minute. Stir in half the parsley, the bay leaf, and the thyme. Add the white wine and cook to reduce it by half.

Add the mussels and cream, cover, and cook, stirring occasionally, for 4 to 5 minutes, or until the mussels have opened. Using a slotted spoon, transfer the mussels to a deep serving dish. Discard any mussels that are not opened. Cover the dish to keep the mussels warm.

Cook the mussel pan juices until reduced by half. Add the remaining parsley and pour the sauce over the mussels.

TO SERVE Place a dish of mussels in the center of the table and let your guests serve themselves, or divide the mussels among individual deep bowls.

This dish has a remarkable depth of earthy tastes. The smoky subtlety of prized morels is poised in perfect equilibrium with the mildly bitter asparagus, to which the cream sauce and puff pastry add a touch of airy elegance. The result is a balance of rustic and refined as satisfying as Europe itself, where these ingredients have been sought after for centuries.

 A recipe such as this calls for a complex wine without too much weight. A classic, crisp counterbalance to the ragout's creaminess might be the Etienne et Daniel Defaix **Chablis** (Chardonnay) Premier Cru from Burgundy, France. A wine that can sweep the palate as well as add dimension to the asparagus notes in the dish is an assertively flavored Marlborough region **Sauvignon Blanc** from New Zealand's Cloudy Bay Winery. If a red is preferred, a bright, spicy Carneros **Pinot Noir** from Robert Sinskey in California's Napa Valley displays this wine's natural affinity to mushrooms.

~ MOREL, ASPARAGUS & CHICKEN RAGOUT ~
in Puff Pastry

Puff Pastry Triangles

8 ounces puff pastry dough

1 egg, beaten with 1 tablespoon water

Morel, Asparagus, and Chicken Ragout

4 ounces skinless, boneless chicken breasts, cut into medium strips

½ teaspoon plus 2 tablespoons unsalted butter

2 shallots, minced

1 garlic clove, minced

8 ounces fresh morels (or 4 ounces dried morels, stemmed, washed, and soaked in warm water for 10 minutes)

Salt & freshly ground white pepper

1 cup heavy cream

1 tablespoon minced fresh flat-leaf (Italian) parsley

8 ounces green asparagus, peeled

Serves 4

CHEF'S NOTES Other mushrooms may be substituted for the morels. When in season, white asparagus may be used instead of green asparagus. The puff pastry triangles can be cooked ahead and kept in an airtight container for up to 5 days.

PREPARATION To make the puff pastry: preheat the oven to 400°F. Line a baking sheet with parchment paper. Roll the puff pastry out on a lightly floured board to a thickness of ⅜ inch. Cut it into two 3½-inch squares, then cut each square in half diagonally to make 4 triangles. Place the triangles on the prepared pan and brush with the egg and water mixture. Bake the puff pastry for about 20 minutes, or until golden brown. Set aside and keep warm.

To make the ragout: blanch the chicken strips in a small saucepan of boiling water for about 1 minute. Drain and set aside. In a medium saucepan, melt the ½ teaspoon butter over medium heat and sauté the shallots and garlic for about 1 minute. Add the morels and sauté for about 1 minute. Season with salt and pepper to taste. Add the cream, reduce heat, and simmer for about 10 minutes. Stir in the chicken and minced parsley and simmer for about 2 minutes. Set aside and keep warm.

Cook the asparagus in salted boiling water until crisp-tender, 3 to 4 minutes. Drain the asparagus and plunge the stalks into a bowl of ice water until cold. Drain again.

Just before serving, melt the 2 tablespoons butter in a large nonstick sauté pan or skillet over medium heat and sauté the asparagus until heated through, about 1 minute. Season with salt and pepper to taste. Set aside and keep warm.

TO SERVE Cut the puff pastry triangles in half horizontally. Place the bottom of a puff pastry triangle in the center of each plate. Top with the chicken mixture. Arrange the asparagus on top of the chicken. Cover with the puff pastry triangle tops and spoon more cream sauce around the puff pastry.

Dairy products are this region's pride, and chicken is vital to the cuisine. At farmers' markets you'll still see cream ladled out of deep vats, and hear the happy cackle of free-range chickens. These age-old specialties form a silky, classic base, to which we add elegant highlights: delicately sweet almonds, a stylish sprinkle of pistachios, and the intense perfume of truffle oil.

 Cream-based soups with earthy elements such as this require a wine that is both dry and complex. Our cellar selection is a classic: a nutty, dry Palomino **Fino Sherry** from Andalusia's Jerez Cortado Hidalgo in southern Spain. For a fruit-forward alternative, Calera's Mount Harlan **Viognier** from California offers perfumed, tropical flavors to add dimension to the earthy character of the soup.

~ CREAM OF CHICKEN SOUP ~
with Truffle Oil

Soup

4 tablespoons unsalted butter

2 shallots, sliced

2 garlic cloves, sliced

⅓ cup all-purpose flour

½ cup dry white wine

6 cups chicken stock (page 159)

Salt & freshly ground white pepper

½ cup heavy cream

3 drops truffle oil

Garnish

½ tablespoon butter

¼ cup finely julienned leek, white part only

2 tablespoons sliced almonds, toasted (page 165)

1 tablespoon pistachios, ground

Serves 4

PREPARATION In a heavy, medium saucepan, melt the butter over medium heat and sauté the shallots and garlic for 2 to 3 minutes, or until translucent. Stir in the flour and cook for about 3 minutes, stirring constantly. Stir in the wine and cook for 1 minute, stirring constantly. Add the stock and bring to a boil. Reduce heat and add the salt and pepper to taste. Add the cream and simmer over very low heat for about 25 minutes, stirring occasionally.

Meanwhile, to make the garnish: using a small sauté pan or skillet, melt the butter over medium heat. Add the leek and sauté for about 1 minute, without coloring. Set aside.

In a blender or food processor, blend the soup until smooth. Strain through a fine-meshed sieve into a soup pot and reheat. Add the truffle oil. Taste and adjust the seasoning.

TO SERVE Ladle into shallow soup bowls and top with the leek, almonds, and pistachios.

This dish was inspired by a visit to the summer cottage of one of our Norwegian captains. The fresh sea smells, singing birds, and bright farmhouses reflected in smooth water were a captivating backdrop, full of culinary inspiration. The result is a textured blend of mild, pure seafood flavors, with herbal highlights and an understated, country-cooking feel — our tribute to the land of the Midnight Sun.

Chowders are substantial and creamy and yet within them lie the subtle, salty flavors of the sea, requiring either refreshing acidity or bright fruit for a complementary balance. A **Sauvignon Blanc** such as Napa Valley's Frog's Leap Winery in California is our cellar selection. It is ripe enough to handle the creamy elements in the broth while the citrus notes gracefully balance the fish flavors. Or for a pairing that offers fruit while still maintaining the necessary crispness, try a dry **Anjou Blanc Sec** (Chenin Blanc blend) from Domaine Ogereau in France's Loire Valley.

3 tablespoons unsalted butter

2 shallots, minced

9 ounces black mussels, scrubbed and debearded

⅓ cup all-purpose flour

3 tablespoons dry white wine

1 teaspoon dry vermouth

3 cups fish stock (page 161)

2 cups water

½ cup heavy cream

1 leek, white part only, cut into fine julienne (¾ cup)

¾ cup finely julienned carrot

¾ cup finely julienned celery

2 ounces salmon fillet, boned, skinned, and cut into ½-inch dice

2 ounces codfish fillet, cut into ½-inch dice

2 Norwegian fish balls (optional)

2 ounces bay shrimp (cooked baby shrimp)

Salt & freshly ground white pepper

1½ tablespoons minced fresh dill

Serves 4

CHEF'S NOTES Norwegian fish balls are a mixture of ground cod, haddock, and whitefish, packed in water. They are available in many import or specialty food stores.

PREPARATION In a soup pot, melt the butter over low heat and sauté the shallots until translucent, about 2 minutes. Add the mussels, increase heat to medium, and sauté for about 2 minutes. Stir in the flour and cook, stirring constantly, for about 2 minutes. Stir in the wine, vermouth, fish stock, and water. Bring to a boil, reduce heat, cover, and simmer for about 3 minutes, or until the mussels have opened. Discard any that have not opened. Using a slotted spoon, transfer the mussels to a bowl. Shell the mussels and set them aside.

Continue to simmer the soup over low heat for about 15 minutes, stirring occasionally. Add the cream and julienned vegetables and simmer for 2 minutes. Add the salmon, cod, and optional fish balls and simmer for 3 minutes. Add the shelled mussels and shrimp and heat for 1 minute. Add the salt and pepper to taste, and the dill.

TO SERVE Ladle into shallow soup bowls.

Norwegians adore fish — and no wonder, with the banquet of tastes and aromas the sea offers up to them. Among their countless superb preparations, some of the best — like this Broiled Salmon — are quite simple, allowing the essential flavors of the fish to emerge. Our chefs use the flavors of spinach and lemon as counterpoints to the richness of the wild salmon steak.

 A rich fish such as salmon requires a wine with depth of fruit and backbone. The Sonoma-Cutrer "Les Pierres Vineyard" **Chardonnay** from California's Sonoma Valley is our top pick, displaying smoke and pear flavors and a lengthy finish. A fruitier style of **Chardonnay**, such as the Willi Bründlmayer from Kamptal, Austria, cleanses the palate with refreshing, toasty apple character. A consummate red wine accompaniment to the salmon is found in the zesty red-berry flavors of Andre Dezat's **Sancerre Rouge** (Pinot Noir) from the Loire Valley of France.

with Creamed Spinach & Sandefjord Butter Sauce

Creamed Spinach

8 cups packed fresh spinach leaves (about 1 bunch)

½ tablespoon unsalted butter

1 small shallot, minced

1 small garlic clove, minced

Salt & freshly ground white pepper

¼ cup heavy cream

¼ cup chicken stock (page 159)

Sandefjord Butter Sauce

3 tablespoons heavy cream

6 tablespoons cold unsalted butter, cut into ½-inch dice

Salt & freshly ground white pepper

½ tablespoon fresh lemon juice

Salmon

4 salmon fillets, 6 ounces each, skinned and boned

1 tablespoon extra-virgin olive oil

Salt & freshly ground white pepper

Garnish

Fresh dill sprigs

Serves 4

CHEF'S NOTES Sandefjord sauce takes its name from the beautiful Sandefjord in Norway where it originated. It is a version of beurre blanc, well known throughout Scandinavia.

PREPARATION To make the Creamed Spinach: blanch the spinach in salted boiling water for 1 minute. Drain, plunge it into ice water, and drain again. Squeeze the spinach between your hands to remove as much water as possible. In a small saucepan, melt the butter over medium heat and sauté the shallots and garlic for about 2 minutes, or until translucent. Stir in the spinach and season with salt and pepper to taste. Stir in the cream and stock and simmer for 2 minutes. In a blender or food processor, purée the mixture until smooth. Set aside and keep warm over hot water.

To make the sauce: bring the cream to a boil in a small, heavy saucepan over medium heat. Remove from heat and gradually whisk in the butter until melted. Add salt and pepper to taste, and the lemon juice. Set aside and keep warm.

Preheat the broiler. Brush the salmon with olive oil and sprinkle with salt and pepper to taste. Place on a broiler pan and broil for 2 to 3 minutes on each side, or until opaque on the outside and slightly translucent in the center.

TO SERVE Pool some creamed spinach in the center of each plate. Arrange the salmon fillets on top of the spinach. Pour the butter sauce around the salmon and spinach. Garnish with dill sprigs.

Savory wild game and tart-sweet forest berries are Scandinavian favorites, especially during the hunting season. We use reindeer from Lapland, where Saami farmers tend their antlered herds as their nomadic ancestors have done for centuries. The lean, distinctive meat, tangy berries, and rich red wine reduction create a stirring harmony of wild and cultivated flavors.

 Strong-flavored game shines against red wine with power and complexity, such as the Guigal **Hermitage Rouge** from the Rhône Valley of France. This wine, vinted entirely from **Syrah**, displays black fruit and peppercorn flavors underscored by firm tannins to balance the venison's robust character. A superb alternative is a traditional **Pauillac** (Cabernet Sauvignon blend), such as the Château Lafite-Rothschild from Bordeaux, France, with black currant fruit flavors and an elegant bouquet. For the same reason, we recommend Opus One **Cabernet Sauvignon blend** from California's Napa Valley, a wine of great depth, with complex oak, sage, spice, and rich berry flavors.

~ ROASTED LOIN OF VENISON ~

with Apple-Lingonberry Relish, Celery Mousseline & Mashed Sweet Potatoes

Sauce

1 tablespoon vegetable oil

About 1 pound venison bones and trimmings, cut up, from loin of venison, below

1 carrot, peeled and chopped

1 small onion, chopped

1 teaspoon cracked black pepper

Salt

2 cups dry red wine

2 cups brown veal stock (page 158)

1 teaspoon Cognac or Brandy

1 tablespoon unsalted butter

Apple-Lingonberry Relish

3 tablespoons finely diced Golden Delicious apple, mixed with 1 teaspoon fresh lemon juice

3 tablespoons lingonberry preserves

Mashed Sweet Potatoes (page 162)

Celery Mousseline

1 small celery root, peeled and cut into ½-inch dice

One ½-inch lemon slice

¼ cup heavy cream

1 teaspoon unsalted butter

Salt & freshly ground white pepper

Venison

One 4-pound rack of venison, boned (bones and trimmings reserved and cut up)

Salt & freshly ground black pepper

½ tablespoon vegetable oil

¼ cup puréed banana

Garnish

Small red currant sprigs

Waffle Potatoes (optional, page 166)

Serves 4

CHEF'S NOTES This traditional European dish may be made with other game. Ask your butcher to bone the loin for you, reserving the bones and trimmings and cutting them into pieces. Cranberry sauce may be substituted for the lingonberry preserves.

PREPARATION To make the sauce: in a stockpot over high heat, heat the oil and brown the venison bones and trimmings on all sides, about 3 minutes. Reduce heat to medium. Add the carrot, onion, and black pepper and sauté for about 3 minutes. Add salt to taste and continue to cook, stirring occasionally, for 3 minutes.

Add the wine and stir to scrape up the browned bits from the bottom of the pan. Cook to reduce by three fourths, 10 to 15 minutes. Add the stock and cook to reduce by half, 15 to 20 minutes. Strain the sauce through a fine-meshed sieve into a small saucepan. Bring the sauce to a boil and add the Cognac or Brandy. Remove from heat and whisk in the butter. Set aside and keep hot.

To make the relish: combine the apple and preserves in a small bowl and stir until blended. Cover and refrigerate.

Prepare the Mashed Sweet Potatoes (page 162).

To make the mousseline: combine the celery and lemon in a small saucepan and add water to cover. Cut a circle of waxed paper to just fit inside the pan and place it on top of the celery. Bring the water to a simmer over medium heat. Cover and cook the celery for about 20 minutes, or until tender.

Drain the celery and remove the lemon slice. Return the pan to the stove and stir the celery constantly over low heat to dry it for about 2 minutes. In a blender or food processor, combine the celery and cream. Add the butter and purée until smooth. Return the mousseline to the saucepan. Add salt and pepper to taste. Set aside and keep warm.

To roast the venison: preheat the oven to 350°F. Sprinkle the venison loin with salt and pepper to taste. In a large nonstick skillet over high heat, heat the oil and sear the loin on both sides until nicely browned, about 1 minute on each side. Put the loin in a roasting pan and roast for about 10 minutes for medium rare (until 130°F). Transfer to a plate and cover loosely with aluminum foil to let rest.

TO SERVE Add the banana purée to the mashed sweet potatoes and stir until thoroughly blended. Pool some red wine sauce in the center of each plate. Cut the meat into 12 equal slices. Place 3 slices in the sauce on each plate. Using 2 soup spoons, form the celery mousseline and mashed sweet potatoes into 4 ovals and place one of each on each plate. Garnish with red currant sprigs and Waffle Potatoes, if using. Drizzle the relish around the meat and serve.

Chef André Soltner is a culinary legend, one of the world's most revered chefs. Using classic French techniques in his own highly personal way, he creates dishes that are worthy of the most refined tables, yet at the same time genuine and human — "real food." This dish is a favorite at his famed New York restaurant, Lutèce, and the Guest Chef Dinners he orchestrates on board.

Roasted fowl is a highly flavorful dish that is best highlighted by a medium-bodied wine with lots of fruit. The Grand Cru "Clos St. Urbain Rangen" **Tokay-Pinot Gris** from Zind-Humbrecht in Alsace is our cellar selection, with its aromatic, floral richness balanced by a crisp frame. The Jaboulet Aîné **Hermitage Blanc** (Marsanne/Roussanne) from the Rhône Valley of France with its elegance and light spice is a fine match. For a superlative red match, the **Pinot Noir** from Benton Lane in Oregon's Willamette Valley delivers tart red fruit flavors to balance the juiciness of the young chicken.

~ ROAST POUSSIN WITH PANACHÉ OF PEAS & CARROTS ~

A recipe from André Soltner

Roast Poussin

2 poussins (baby chickens), about
1 pound each

1 teaspoon salt

½ teaspoon freshly ground black pepper

4 fresh thyme sprigs

5 fresh tarragon sprigs

4 fresh parsley sprigs

2 small onions

2 teaspoons peanut oil

Panaché of Peas and Carrots

2 tablespoons unsalted butter

1 small onion, thinly sliced

2 small carrots, peeled and cut into
⅛-inch-thick disks

1 pound small young green peas, shelled

Leaves from ½ small head Boston
(butter) lettuce, cut into ¼-inch-wide
ribbons

½ teaspoon sugar

Salt & freshly ground white pepper

½ cup chicken stock (page 159)
or water

⅛ cup heavy cream

1 tablespoon chopped fresh chervil
or parsley

Sauce

¼ cup dry white wine

¼ cup chicken stock (page 159)

2 tablespoons minced fresh flat-leaf
(Italian) parsley

1 tablespoon unsalted butter

Garnish

Fresh rosemary sprigs

Serves 2-4

CHEF'S NOTES Of all of my dishes, the recipe for this simple and very popular chicken dish is asked for the most often by food writers and others. We have served it at Lutèce every day since we opened.

PREPARATION To roast the poussins: preheat the oven to 450°F. Wash the poussins inside and out with cold running water and pat them dry with paper towels. Sprinkle the poussins inside and out with the salt and pepper.

Put 2 thyme sprigs, 2 tarragon sprigs, 2 parsley sprigs, and 1 onion in the body cavity of each poussin. Truss the poussins with kitchen twine. Strip the leaves from the remaining tarragon sprig and set them aside.

In a heavy roasting pan just large enough to hold the poussins, heat the oil over high heat and brown the poussins on all sides. Put the pan in the oven and roast, breast-side up, basting every 5 minutes with any pan juices until the poussins are crisp and golden brown, 20 to 25 minutes. (Note: it is a good idea to throw 1 or 2 tablespoons of hot water in the oven, to create steam, after each basting. This will keep the poussins moist.)

Meanwhile, make the panaché: in a medium, heavy saucepan, melt the butter over medium-low heat and sauté the onion for about 3 minutes, or until translucent. Add the carrots, peas, lettuce, sugar, and salt and pepper to taste. Cover, reduce heat to low, and cook for 10 minutes, stirring several times. Add the stock or water and bring to a boil. Cover, reduce heat to low, and cook for 10 minutes, stirring once or twice. Add the cream and cook, uncovered, until the liquid begins to thicken, about 5 minutes, stirring once or twice. Sprinkle with the chervil or parsley.

To make the sauce: remove the roasting pan from the oven, transfer the poussins to a serving platter, and cover them loosely with aluminum foil. Pour off the fat from the pan and put the pan over medium heat. Add the wine and stir to scrape up the browned bits from the bottom of the pan. Add the stock, reserved tarragon leaves, and parsley. Simmer for 2 minutes. Remove the pan from heat and stir in the butter. Set aside and keep warm.

TO SERVE Place the poussins on warm plates, pour the pan sauce around them, and garnish with fresh rosemary sprigs. Accompany with the panaché alongside. Serve immediately.

As your Head Waiter carves this Rack of Veal at the tableside, you sense that you are about to enjoy something very special, and then the first morsel exceeds your highest expectations. The tender, marinated meat, with the complex vegetal flavors of the celery gratin and crowned by earthy potatoes, leeks, and the aromatic warmth of herbs, form a stately mélange of taste and texture.

Tender meat dishes accentuated by the clean flavors of resinous herbs are beautifully offset by medium-bodied reds or whites with strong character. Our cellar selection has the elegance that veal requires, yet displays smoky and tobacco-leaf notes: Marchese Antinori's Tignanello (**Sangiovese/Cabernet Sauvignon**) from Tuscany, Italy. A softer alternative can be found in the red cherry flavors of the Markham **Merlot** from Napa Valley in California. The toasty aromas and rich texture of a Chardonnay, such as the Ampeau **Meursault** from France's Burgundy region, are exquisite as well.

~ ROASTED RACK OF VEAL ~
with Potato, Leek & Celery Gratin

Marinated Veal

2 tablespoons extra-virgin olive oil

1 tablespoon minced fresh thyme

1 tablespoon minced fresh rosemary

1 rack of veal, with 6 ribs, Frenched
(trimmings reserved)

Potato, Leek, and Celery Gratin

1½ tablespoons extra-virgin olive oil

1 small shallot, finely sliced

2 small garlic cloves, finely sliced

⅓ leek, white part only, finely sliced

1 teaspoon minced fresh thyme

1 small celery root, peeled, halved
horizontally, and cut into ⅛-inch-thick
vertical slices

1 large (10-ounce) boiling potato,
peeled, halved horizontally, and cut into
⅛-inch-thick vertical slices

Salt & freshly ground white pepper

1 cup milk

½ cup heavy cream

¾ cup (3 ounces) shredded
Gruyère cheese

Sauce

Salt & freshly ground white pepper

2 tablespoons extra-virgin olive oil

Reserved veal bones and trimmings

1 onion, cut into ¾-inch dice

½ unpeeled head garlic

1 carrot, cut into ¾-inch dice

1 celery stalk, cut into ¾-inch dice

2 fresh thyme sprigs

1 small fresh rosemary sprig

1 bay leaf

2 cups dry white wine

3 cups of water

1 tablespoon flour

½ tablespoon tomato paste

Serves 6

CHEF'S NOTES Ask your butcher to French the veal rack and to reserve the trimmings and the bones. The veal should be marinated for at least 4 hours, or preferably overnight.

PREPARATION To marinate the veal: combine the oil and herbs in a glass baking dish. Add the veal, turn to coat, cover, and refrigerate for at least 4 hours. Remove from the refrigerator and let sit at room temperature while making the gratin.

To make the gratin: preheat the oven to 350°F. In a large nonstick sauté pan or skillet over medium heat, heat 1 tablespoon of the olive oil and sauté the shallot, garlic, leek, and thyme for about 2 minutes. Add the celery root and potato and sauté for about 2 more minutes, stirring constantly. Season with salt and pepper to taste. Add the milk and cream, reduce heat, and simmer for about 5 minutes. Brush a gratin dish with the remaining ½ tablespoon olive oil. Place the gratin mixture in the dish and sprinkle with the Gruyère. Bake for about 30 minutes, or until the gratin is golden brown and the potatoes are tender when pierced with a knife. Remove the gratin from the oven and keep warm. Leave the oven on.

To roast the veal: sprinkle the veal rack with salt and pepper. In a large ovenproof sauté pan or skillet over high heat, heat the oil and sear the veal rack, bone-side down, until lightly browned, 1 to 2 minutes. Turn over and sear on the second side for 1 to 2 minutes. Transfer the veal rack to a plate. Heat the same pan over high heat, add the veal bones and trimmings, and sear until browned, about 3 minutes. Reduce heat to medium and add the onion, garlic, carrot, celery, and herbs. Cook, stirring constantly, for about 3 minutes. Season with salt and pepper to taste. Spoon off the excess fat from the pan. Add 1 cup of the wine and stir to scrape up the browned bits from the bottom of the pan. Place the veal rack on top of the sautéed bones and vegetables and roast in the oven for about 15 minutes. Add 1 cup of water, turn the veal rack, and roast for about 15 more minutes for medium; a thermometer will register 140°F. Remove the pan from the oven, transfer the veal rack to a plate, cover loosely with aluminum foil, and let rest.

To make the sauce: return the pan with the bones and vegetables to medium heat, add the flour and the tomato paste, and cook, stirring constantly, for about 1 minute. Add the remaining 1 cup wine and cook for about 2 minutes. Add the remaining water and return to a boil. Reduce heat to low and simmer until the liquid is reduced by two thirds, about 25 minutes. Strain through a fine-meshed sieve into a small saucepan. Taste and adjust the seasoning. Set the sauce aside and keep warm.

TO SERVE Cut the rack into 6 chops. Pool sauce in the center of each plate. Place a chop on each plate and and serve some of the gratin alongside. Pour more sauce over the chops.

This dish features two Austrian hallmarks: pork and horseradish. Pork in all its variations — chops, roasts, hams, rillettes, sausages, and patés — is a central European passion, while the pepperiness of horseradish is as familiar in Austrian cooking as ginger is in China. Slow-cooked potatoes and other root vegetables, cornichons, and mustard complete this classic European recipe.

A dish that exhibits a full range of flavors from spicy and tangy to sweet begs a wine with equal intensity and fruit, yet without drying tannins. For our cellar selection, we chose Austria's Albert Neumeister "Saziani Selection" **Grauburgunder** (Pinot Gris) from Straden, which calms the strong flavors with its floral, aromatic qualities. A flattering accompaniment is found in the citrusy/smoky flavors of the Franciscan "Cuvée Sauvage" **Chardonnay**, from Napa Valley, California. From Piedmont, Italy, the Aldo Conterno **Dolcetto d'Alba**, displays red fruit and bracing acidity to contrast this dish's range of sweet and spicy flavors.

~ HORSERADISH-BASTED PORK TENDERLOIN ~
with Potatoes Rösti

Pork Tenderloin

Two 10-ounce pork tenderloins, trimmed of all visible fat

Salt & freshly ground white pepper

½ tablespoon vegetable oil

1½ tablespoons dried bread crumbs

12 bacon slices, blanched and drained

Horseradish Crust

4 tablespoons prepared horseradish

2 tablespoons flour

1 egg yolk

2 tablespoons heavy cream

Freshly ground white pepper

Sauce

1 shallot, minced

2 tablespoons white wine vinegar

½ cup dry white wine

Bouquet garni (page 158)

½ teaspoon cracked black pepper

2 cups brown veal stock (page 158)

2 teaspoons Dijon mustard

2 tablespoons unsalted butter

2 tablespoons cornichons, julienned

Salt & freshly ground black pepper

Potatoes Rösti

2 large russet potatoes, about 10 ounces each, cooked half-way through and peeled

1 leek, white part only, julienned

Salt & freshly ground white pepper

1 tablespoon minced fresh flat-leaf (Italian) parsley

2½ tablespoons vegetable oil

2 tablespoons clarified butter (page 160)

Garnish

Chive blossoms and fresh sage leaves

Serves 4

CHEF'S NOTES Pork tenderloins can be substituted with chicken breasts. Potatoes Rösti is a traditional pan-fried dish from Switzerland. They can be substituted with hash brown potatoes.

PREPARATION To cook the pork: preheat the oven to 375°F. Sprinkle the tenderloins with salt and pepper to taste. In a large sauté pan or skillet over high heat, heat the oil and sear the tenderloins on all sides for about 2 minutes, or until nicely golden brown. Transfer to paper towels.

Line a cutting board with a 10-by-12-inch piece of aluminum foil. Sprinkle the foil with half the bread crumbs and place 6 bacon strips side by side on top of the crumbs. In a small bowl, mix all the crust ingredients together, using the pepper to taste. Spread half of the crust mixture evenly over one of the tenderloins. Place the tenderloin on the foil at one end, at a 45-degree angle to the bacon strips. Roll the foil with the bacon around the tenderloin and tie it closed in several places with kitchen string. Repeat with the second tenderloin. Place the wrapped tenderloins in a roasting pan and roast in the oven for about 15 minutes. Remove the tenderloins from the oven and let them rest in the foil. Leave the oven set at 375°F.

To make the sauce: combine the shallot, vinegar, wine, bouquet garni, and pepper in a small saucepan. Bring to a boil over medium heat and cook to reduce by three fourths, then discard the bouquet garni. Add the stock and cook to reduce by two thirds. Remove from heat and whisk in the mustard and butter. Add the cornichons and season with salt and pepper to taste. Set aside and keep warm.

To cook the potatoes: shred the potatoes on the large holes of a four-sided grater and put in a bowl. Add the leek, salt and pepper to taste, and parsley and mix well. In a small, nonstick sauté pan or skillet over medium heat, heat ½ tablespoon oil with ½ tablespoon butter. Add one fourth of the potato mixture and flatten with a metal spatula. Cook for 4 to 5 minutes, or until golden brown on the bottom. Flip over and cook for 4 to 5 minutes on the second side, or until golden brown. Put the potato cake on a baking sheet. Repeat with the remaining potato mixture to make 4 cakes. Bake the cakes in the 375°F oven for 5 minutes.

Remove the foil from the wrapped tenderloins. In a large nonstick sauté pan or skillet over medium heat, heat the remaining ½ tablespoon oil and brown the wrapped tenderloins on all sides for about 2 minutes, or until the bacon is golden brown and lightly crisp. Cut each tenderloin into 6 medallions.

TO SERVE Place a potato cake in the center of each plate. Place 3 slices of tenderloin on top of each potato cake and pour the sauce around the cake. Garnish with the chive blossoms and sage leaves and serve at once.

The beauty, tartness, and bewitching sweetness of berries are the keynote of many European desserts. Here, glazed raspberries sit like gleaming jewels in a golden crown of sweet pastry, their wild, robust flavors soothed by the silkiness of the lemon cream. Perfect to conclude a casual meal, or to nibble with a warming cappuccino as you look over a glassy blue fjord.

The melding of this dessert's tart-berry flavors creates an incomparably delicious pairing with wines that show refreshing high notes layered over intense fruit character. Our cellar selection, the Robert Mondavi "Muscato d'Oro" (**Muscat Canelli**), from Napa Valley, California, reveals an intoxicating balancing act of spice, floral notes, and sweet citrus fruit, an excellent example of a truly balanced dessert wine. From across the Atlantic we find a classic Italian match to the berries and smooth cream in the sparkling, delicately peachy Martini & Rossi **Asti Spumanti** (Muscat Canelli) from Piedmont.

with Wild Forest Berries

Sweet Pastry Crust

1¾ cups all-purpose flour

Pinch of salt

⅓ cup sugar

4 egg yolks

⅛ teaspoon vanilla extract

½ cup (1 stick) cold unsalted butter, cut into small pieces

Lemon Cream

4 egg yolks

½ cup sugar

1 cup milk

1 envelope plain gelatin

Grated zest of 1 lemon, blanched (page 158), 8 curls reserved for garnish

Juice of 1 lemon

1 cup heavy cream, whipped

6 ounces dark chocolate, melted

Berry Filling

4 cups fresh raspberries

¼ cup raspberry jelly

1 teaspoon plain gelatin

Garnish

¼ cup pistachios, ground

8 lemon zest curls, reserved from above

Makes 8 individual tarts

PREPARATION To make the crust: in a medium bowl, stir the flour, salt, and sugar together. Stir in the egg yolks and vanilla extract until blended. Add the butter and work it into the flour mixture with your fingers until the mixture resembles coarse crumbs. Using a dough scraper or spatula, mix the dough with a cutting motion until smooth.

Turn the dough out on a lightly floured board and, using the heel of one hand, push it away in small portions until all the dough has been smeared. Gather the dough up with a dough scraper or spatula and press the dough into a ball. Wrap in plastic wrap and refrigerate for at least 30 minutes or up to 3 days.

Roll the dough out to a 13-inch circle. Using a 5-inch round cookie cutter, cut out 8 rounds. Fit each into a 3-inch tartlet mold. Pierce the bottom of the crust all over with a fork. Fit a piece of parchment paper into each crust and fill with dried beans or pie weights. Bake the crusts for 15 minutes, or until lightly browned. Let cool on a wire rack.

To make the Lemon Cream: in a medium bowl, beat the egg yolks with ¼ cup of the sugar until thickened and pale in color. In a small saucepan, combine the milk, remaining ¼ cup sugar, and gelatin and bring to a boil. Gradually whisk the milk mixture into the yolk mixture. Return to the saucepan and cook, stirring constantly, until bubbles form around the edges of the pan. Strain the mixture through a fine-meshed sieve into a bowl. Refrigerate until cool and beginning to thicken, about 15 minutes. Stir in the blanched lemon zest and lemon juice until blended. Fold in the whipped cream until thoroughly blended.

ASSEMBLY Using a pastry brush, coat the inside of the pastry shells with a thin layer of chocolate. Allow the chocolate to set. Then, pour the cream into the tart shells and refrigerate for 15 minutes. Arrange the berries in a pattern on top of the cream. Combine the raspberry jelly with the gelatin. With a brush, coat the berries with the raspberry jelly mixture. Pat the ground pistachios around the edges of the tarts. Garnish with reserved lemon zest.

Mozart Tea in the Palm Court has become a Crystal institution, and this Kirschtorte explains why. The rich cream and dense, dark chocolate blend with the sweetly sour cherries. Enjoyed in a landscape of palm trees and luminous sea views, with waiters in period costumes of velvet and lace, our extravagant cake returns you to the golden age of eighteenth-century Vienna.

 For a dessert that rides the line between tartness and richness, a wine such as the Schloss Saarstein Estate "Serriger" **Eiswein** (Riesling), from the Mosel-Saar-Ruwer region of Germany, is a superb choice. Its lush, honeyed apricot character, balanced by fine acidity, makes it our cellar selection for this dessert. California's Joseph Phelps' "Délice" **Late Harvest Semillon** from the Napa Valley, with sweet fig and peach flavors, is also a delicious, equally rich match for the Kirschtorte.

Chocolate Génoise Cake (page 159)

Cherry Filling

¼ cup water

¼ cup granulated sugar

Pinch of ground cinnamon

6 ounces canned whole sour cherries, drained and pitted

Kirsch Syrup

¼ cup kirsch liqueur

¼ cup granulated sugar

Chocolate Cream

1 tablespoon water

2 ounces semisweet chocolate, chopped

½ cup heavy cream, whipped

Kirsch Cream

3 tablespoons confectioners' sugar

3 tablespoons kirsch

1 cup heavy cream

Garnish

½ cup heavy cream, whipped

8 pitted fresh Bing cherries or candied cherries

2 ounces semisweet chocolate, shaved

Makes one 8-inch cake, serves 8

CHEF'S NOTES For the best texture, make the génoise 1 day before assembling the cake. Use top-quality kirsch, preferably from Bavaria or Switzerland.

PREPARATION Prepare the Chocolate Génoise Cake (page 159).

To make the Cherry Filling: in a small saucepan, combine the water and sugar. Bring to a boil and cook for about 5 minutes, or until the sugar is dissolved and the mixture is slightly thickened. Reduce heat to very low, add the remaining filling ingredients, and simmer for 2 minutes. Set aside to cool.

To make the Kirsch Syrup: combine the kirsch and sugar in a small saucepan and bring to a boil. Reduce heat to low and simmer for about 5 minutes, or until the sugar is dissolved.

To make the Chocolate Cream: combine the water and chocolate in a double boiler and melt over barely simmering water. Set aside until cooled to room temperature but not set. Gradually fold the whipped cream into the chocolate.

To make the Kirsch Cream: combine all the ingredients in a deep bowl and beat until stiff peaks form.

ASSEMBLY Cut the cake into 3 equal layers. Using a pastry brush, soak the first layer of cake with one third of the syrup. Spread this layer with the Chocolate Cream. Top with the Cherry Filling. Place a second layer of cake on top and gently press it down. Soak the second cake layer with one third of the syrup, and top with half of the Kirsch Cream. Add the third layer of cake and gently press it down. Soak this layer with the remaining syrup. Refrigerate for about 3 hours to set the fillings.

Using an icing spatula, coat the cake evenly on the top and sides with the remining Kirsch Cream. Fit a pastry bag with a No. 10 star tip and fill it with the whipped cream. Pipe 8 rosettes of whipped cream, spacing them evenly around the top of the cake. Place a cherry on top of each rosette. Sprinkle the chocolate shavings over the cake.

Legend has it that when the Turks besieged Vienna, a baker inside the city walls made this cake in the shape of their hats. In the time he took to make the dough, let it rise, and bake the cake, the Austrian army defeated the invading Turks, leaving the townspeople free to enjoy his stylish new dessert. There are many variations on this prized recipe; ours is simple and delicious, with raisins.

Cakes with fruit baked into them are particularly delectable with an off-dry yet crisp wine such as our cellar selection, the "Cuvée Frédérick Émile, Sélection de Grains Nobles" **Riesling** from Trimbach in Alsace, France. A delicious sparkling wine to try with this dessert is the Louis Roederer **Grand Vin Sec Champagne** from France, which shows a delicate sweetness that stands up to the nutty, fruity character of the cake.

Gugelhopf

⅓ cup raisins

⅜ cup warm (105° to 115°F) milk

2 packages active dried yeast

1½ cups all-purpose flour

¼ cup granulated sugar

½ teaspoon salt

3 egg yolks

Grated zest of ½ lemon

⅓ cup unsalted butter, at room temperature

¼ cup sliced almonds, toasted (page 165)

Garnish

Confectioners' sugar for dusting

Fresh strawberries

Makes one 9-inch bundt cake, serves 8

CHEF'S NOTES The dough may be made 1 day in advance and refrigerated; this gives the cake a fine texture. The cake may also be served warm, with Crème Anglaise (page 160).

PREPARATION Butter and flour a 9-inch-diameter, 4¼-inch-high bundt pan. In a small bowl, combine the raisins with warm water to cover. Set aside to soak.

In a small bowl, stir the milk and yeast together and let sit for about 5 minutes, or until creamy. In a large bowl, stir the flour, sugar, and salt together. Using a heavy-duty mixer fitted with the plastic paddle, or using a wooden spoon, mix in the yeast mixture. Immediately mix in the egg yolks and lemon zest until thoroughly blended. Mix in the butter until thoroughly blended. Continue to stir until the dough forms a ball around the dough hook or pulls away from the sides of the bowl. If the dough is too stiff, add a little milk.

Drain the raisins. Using the mixer, mix in the raisins and almonds until evenly dispersed throughout the dough. Or, put the dough on a lightly floured surface and knead in the raisins and almonds with your hands.

Put the dough in the prepared pan. Cover with plastic wrap and let rise in a warm place until doubled in volume, about 2 hours.

Preheat the oven to 375°F. Bake the cake for 30 to 35 minutes, or until a skewer inserted in the cake comes out clean. Unmold the cake onto a wire rack and let cool.

TO SERVE Place the cake on a cake plate and dust with confectioners' sugar. Cut into wedges and garnish with strawberries.

This fluffy soufflé is one of our pâtissiers' best kept secrets, and among their most requested desserts. It originated in Salzburg, and is near and dear to every Austrian's heart—"sweet as cream, tender as a kiss," as they like to describe them. Its soft, sweet peaks remind our Austrian pastry chefs of their beloved snow-clad Alps, where warm family homes await them.

Elegant desserts demand elegant wines as complements, and our cellar selection, the Kracher "Grand Cuvée" **Eiswein** (Chardonnay/ Welschriesling) from Neusiedlersee in Austria, rises to meet this airy dessert with true honeyed elegance. If bubbles are in order, a **Rosé Brut Champagne** from Laurent Perrier of France will highlight the strawberry flavors and freshness of the dessert without overwhelming its delicacy.

~ SALZBURGER NOCKERLN ~
with Strawberry Cream

Soufflé

8 egg whites at room temperature

⅔ cup granulated sugar

2 egg yolks, beaten

⅛ teaspoon vanilla extract

2 tablespoons lingonberry preserves

Strawberry Cream

1 cup heavy cream

*2 tablespoons Strawberry Coulis
(page 164)*

*1 tablespoon Grand Marnier or other
orange liqueur*

Garnish

Confectioners' sugar for dusting

Serves 4

CHEF'S NOTES This traditional Austrian dessert should be served hot from the oven, with the strawberry cream alongside. Hot chocolate sauce may be substituted for the strawberry cream. Strawberry preserves may be substituted for the lingonberry preserves.

PREPARATION To make the soufflé: preheat the oven to 400°F. In a large bowl, beat the egg whites until soft peaks form. Gradually beat the sugar into the egg whites until stiff, glossy peaks form. Beat about one fourth of the méringue into the egg yolks. Fold the egg yolk mixture and vanilla into the remaining méringue until blended.

Grease an ovenproof oval ceramic platter or baking dish, about 12 inches long, with soft butter and dust with sugar. Spoon the preserves into the platter or into the baking dish and spread them evenly over the bottom.

Using a large spoon, scoop 4 large mounds of the méringue onto the platter or into the dish. Bake for about 15 minutes, or until lightly browned.

Meanwhile, make the Strawberry Cream: in a deep bowl, beat the cream until stiff peaks form. Fold in the coulis and liqueur until blended.

TO SERVE Using a large spoon, transfer each nockerln to a dessert plate. Dust the nockerln with confectioners' sugar. Serve at once, with the strawberry cream alongside.

Tropical Rhythms Everywhere you hear

the music of this great land, feel its energy and love of life. Carnaval dancers swirl to the hypnotic beat of samba and calypso,

gauchos ride the rolling plains of the Pampas, a cliff diver soars through the clear blue air. Yet beneath the lively emotions lie age-old refinements, brought here by European explorers and settlers centuries ago. Nowhere is this blend of traditions more exciting than in the local cuisine, a perfect marriage of New World spirit and Old World style. From the sun-warmed soil grow fiery chilies, succulent tropical fruits, dark, rich chocolate and coffee. Cattle graze on lush grasslands, while the warm Pacific and the chill Antarctic harbor a wealth of deep-sea fish and crustaceans. To these robust flavors, Europeans have added olive oil, legumes, herbs, and cooking techniques used with a Mediterranean flair; desserts with a Central European richness and subtlety. In each of our recipes, the passion and polish of local cuisine go hand in hand. Tempering the dynamic flavors of the region with their own European finesse, our chefs create their personal vision of Latin America and the Caribbean.

"The cuisine of this region fits the energy
of the land and its people, earthy and full of passion.
The infusion of European immigrants adds a classical touch."
—*Toni Neumeister*

This dish has a spirited history, and expresses our culinary philosophy in a few elegant morsels. Born in Spain as a cold marinade for preserving cooked foods, escabeche crossed the Atlantic with European travelers and is now cherished throughout South America. Our version is painted in the fresh, bright colors of the New World, yet its balanced flavors have a European elegance.

Seafood dishes that highlight sweet herbal flavors such as fennel have a great affinity to aromatic, dry white wines. Our cellar selection, the Errazuriz **Sauvignon Blanc** from the Casablanca Valley in Chile, shows mouth-watering flavors of tropical fruit and citrus. The Columbia Crest **Johannisberg Riesling**, from Washington's Columbia Valley, picks up on the sweetness of the fennel with its ripe peach and floral character. The Louis Michel et Fils **Chablis** (Chardonnay) from Burgundy, France, displays a stony, citrus affinity to the lime notes in the sauce.

～ ESCABECHE OF PRAWNS ～
with Braised Saffron Fennel

Escabeche

2 tablespoons olive oil

2 shallots, minced

1 carrot, peeled and finely diced

1 celery stalk, peeled and finely diced

4 garlic cloves, halved lengthwise

Salt & freshly ground pepper

3 cups chicken stock (page 159)

¼ cup sherry vinegar

4 small bay leaves

4 fresh thyme sprigs

12 saffron threads

Pinch of cayenne pepper

12 jumbo shrimp, peeled and deveined, tails left on

Braised Saffron Fennel

1 tablespoon extra-virgin olive oil

1 fennel bulb, trimmed and cut into thin lengthwise slices

Salt & freshly ground white pepper

1 garlic clove, minced

¼ cup dry white wine

12 threads saffron

1 cup stock from shrimp, above

Vinaigrette

Liquid from fennel and shrimp, above

2 tablespoons extra-virgin olive oil

Juice of 1 fresh lime

1 tablespoon chopped fresh flat-leaf (Italian) parsley

1 large tomato, peeled, seeded, and diced (page 163)

Garnish

Fresh fennel sprigs and borage blossoms

Serves 4

CHEF'S NOTES The flavor of this dish will be even better if the prawns and fennel are prepared 1 day ahead and refrigerated overnight. Use only top-quality extra-virgin olive oil for the most flavorful results.

PREPARATION To make the Escabeche: in a heavy, medium stockpot over medium heat, heat the oil and sauté the shallots for about 3 minutes, or until translucent. Add the carrot, celery, and garlic and sauté for 2 minutes. Add salt and pepper to taste, stock, vinegar, bay leaves, thyme, saffron, and cayenne. Bring to a boil, reduce heat, and simmer for 5 minutes. Add the shrimp and bring to a boil; reduce heat, cover, and simmer for about 2 minutes, or until the shrimp are pink and opaque. Transfer the shrimp and the liquid to a bowl, and reserve the bay leaves, thyme sprigs, and garlic for garnish. Cover the shrimp and refrigerate for at least 4 hours or overnight.

To braise the fennel: in a medium sauté pan or skillet, over high heat, heat the oil and sauté the fennel for 1 minute. Add salt and pepper to taste and the garlic, and sauté for 1 minute. Add the wine and saffron. Cook, stirring, until the wine is reduced to about 1 tablespoon. Pour off 1 cup of the reserved shrimp stock, add to the fennel, and cook for 2 minutes. Remove from heat and transfer to a bowl. Cover and refrigerate for at least 3 hours or overnight.

Remove the shrimp and fennel from the refrigerator. Using a slotted spoon, remove the fennel from its liquid and divide the fennel among the plates. Using a slotted spoon, remove the shrimp from its liquid and place 3 on each plate.

To make the vinaigrette: pour the fennel liquid into the shrimp liquid. Stir in the olive oil, lime juice, parsley, and chopped tomato. Taste and adjust the seasoning.

TO SERVE Arrange braised fennel in the center of each plate with 3 shrimp around it. Spoon the vinaigrette over each serving. Garnish with the bay leaves, thyme sprigs, and garlic reserved from the Escabeche preparation, along with fennel sprigs and borage blossoms as desired.

Crab cakes are a Latin American specialty. Some of the tastiest are made from crabs caught in freezing Antarctic waters off South America, famous for seafood. Though the waters are cold, the land and its people are fiery and passionate. So we created a spicy salsa to complement these delicately flavored cakes, with papaya that lends a unique tropical accent.

 While crab is fairly rich, it is the sweetness of the peppers and the intensity of the spices that set the tone for this dish. We suggest a **Riesling**, such as the Hermann J. Wiemer from the Finger Lakes region in New York, which displays fruitiness combined with acidity to stand up to both the spice notes and the textural roundness of the crab. For a southern hemisphere alternative, the Casa Lapostolle **Chardonnay** from the Rapel Valley in Chile delivers complex toast notes and ripe fruit. One finds the same richness and fruit-forward flavors in the ZD **Chardonnay** from the Napa Valley, California.

∼ CRAB CAKES ∼
with Salsa de Crystal

Salsa de Crystal

½ *small red onion, finely chopped*

1 *garlic clove, minced*

Juice of 2 limes

10 *fresh cilantro sprigs*

5 *tomatoes, peeled, seeded, and finely chopped (page 163)*

½ *cup finely diced papaya*

2 *tablespoons extra-virgin olive oil*

Pinch of cayenne pepper

Pinch of ground cumin

Salt & freshly ground white pepper

Crab Cakes

½ *teaspoon extra-virgin olive oil*

½ *onion, very finely chopped*

⅓ *celery stalk, peeled and diced*

2 *small garlic cloves, minced*

8 *ounces fresh lump crabmeat*

½ *small red bell pepper, seeded, deribbed, and finely diced*

½ *small green bell pepper, seeded, deribbed, and finely diced*

1 *green onion, finely chopped, including green portions*

3 *tablespoons mayonnaise (page 163)*

½ *tablespoon Creole mustard*

2 *cups fresh bread crumbs*

Pinch of cayenne pepper

Salt & freshly ground white pepper

1 *egg, lightly beaten*

1 *teaspoon clarified unsalted butter (page 160)*

Salad Garnish

2 *cups mixed salad greens*

1 *tablespoon fresh lemon juice*

1 *tablespoon extra-virgin olive oil*

Salt & freshly ground white pepper

Serves 4

CHEF'S NOTES The salsa improves in flavor if made 1 day before serving. The homemade mayonnaise may be replaced by a good-quality commercial brand. A spicy vinaigrette or mayonnaise may be substituted for the salsa.

PREPARATION To make the salsa: in a small bowl, combine all the ingredients, using salt and pepper to taste, and stir to mix. Cover and refrigerate for at least 2 hours, or preferably overnight.

To make the crab cakes: in a small sauté pan or skillet over low heat, heat the olive oil and sauté the onion, celery, and garlic until the onion is translucent, about 3 minutes. Set aside and let cool.

In a small bowl, combine the crabmeat, bell peppers, green onion, and sautéed onion mixture. Add the mayonnaise, mustard, 1 cup of the bread crumbs, the cayenne, and salt and pepper to taste. Stir to blend. Divide the mixture into 8 equal parts and form into cakes 2½ inches in diameter and ½ inch thick.

Place the beaten egg and the remaining bread crumbs in separate shallow bowls. Coat each cake with the beaten egg, then the bread crumbs.

In a large nonstick sauté pan or skillet, heat the clarified butter over medium heat and fry the cakes for about 2 minutes on each side. Using a slotted metal spatula, transfer the cakes to paper towels to drain.

TO SERVE Toss the greens with the lemon juice and oil, and season with salt and pepper to taste. Place 2 crab cakes in the center of each plate. Garnish with the salad. Serve at once with the salsa alongside.

When the explorers came to the New World, they found a treasure trove of new foods. They also brought favorite ingredients from Europe, and cooking on both sides of the Atlantic was changed forever. Our soup salutes this gastronomic revolution, joining Spain's cold gazpacho with tomatoes and avocados from the Americas, with a refined French classic touch in the preparation.

 Soups such as this which offer the duality of refreshing acidity from the tomatoes and cooling richness of the avocado require a wine that has a dry, fine fruit character. For our cellar selection we chose the Chalk Hill **Sauvignon Blanc** from the Alexander Valley of Sonoma County, California. The sweet oak and citrus high notes meet the soup and complement the basil and tomato flavors. A wonderful alternative is the fruity and off-dry Viña Cunqueiro **Ribeiro Blanco** (Treixandura/Torrontés) from Galicia, Spain. Its full style enhances the fruitiness of the tomato and fennel flavors with a fresh clean finish.

~ CHILLED TOMATO-BASIL SOUP ~
with Avocado Tartare

Soup

1 tablespoon extra-virgin olive oil

1 small onion, finely chopped

1½ shallots, minced

2 garlic cloves, minced

1 small leek, white part only, coarsely chopped

½ red bell pepper, seeded, deribbed, and finely diced

⅓ cup finely diced fennel

⅓ cup chopped fresh basil

1 tablespoon tomato paste

4 cups chicken stock (page 159)

1½ pounds tomatoes, peeled, seeded, and coarsely chopped (page 163)

1 cup tomato juice

Tabasco sauce

Salt & freshly ground white pepper

Avocado Tartare

2 ripe avocados, peeled, pitted, and chopped

1 small shallot, chopped

1 garlic clove, chopped

6 fresh cilantro sprigs, chopped

Tabasco sauce

Salt & freshly ground white pepper

Garnish

Fresh basil sprigs

Serves 6

CHEF'S NOTES This soup is best in summer when tomatoes are at their most flavorful. It can be made 1 day ahead, but the avocado tartare should be made right before serving to prevent it from discoloring.

PREPARATION In a heavy, medium soup pot over low heat, heat the olive oil and sauté the onion, shallots, garlic, leek, bell pepper, and fennel for about 4 minutes. Add the basil and tomato paste and sauté for 1 minute. Add 2 cups of the chicken stock. Pour into a blender or food processor and blend until smooth. Return to the pot and add the tomatoes, tomato juice, and remaining 2 cups stock. Cover and simmer for about 25 minutes.

In a blender or food processor, blend the soup until smooth. Strain the soup through a fine-meshed sieve, pressing on the solids with the back of a large spoon. Add Tabasco and salt and pepper to taste. Refrigerate the soup for at least 2 hours, or preferably overnight.

To make the tartare: just before serving, combine the avocado, shallot, garlic, and cilantro in a small bowl and stir to mix. Season with Tabasco and salt and pepper to taste.

TO SERVE Using 2 soup spoons, form the tartare into 6 ovals and place 1 in the center of each of 6 shallow soup bowls. Pour the chilled soup around the tartare (the avocado tartare quenelles should not be completely covered with soup) and garnish the rim of each bowl with a basil sprig.

An afternoon in a South American port is a feast of the senses, and a solace for the spirit. In the quiet of afternoon siesta time, the aroma of corn roasting on open fires floats on the breeze; shiny braids of chilies hang drying in the sun. Such tastes and emotions infuse this soup, with its balance of sweet, lightly smoky corn, cooling cream, and the chili's gentle fire.

Because the base of this dish is corn, one needs to match it with a similarly weighted wine, such as a Chardonnay. Our cellar selection is from the Casablanca Valley of Chile: the Concha y Toro **Chardonnay**, which balances the sweet corn flavors with assertive, rich fruit. Because the soup also presents a roasted flavor, the nutty, crisp character of the Domaine Chandon **Brut Cuvée Sparkling Wine** (Méthode Champenoise) from California's Napa Valley is a superb contrast for this soup.

~ ROASTED CORN SOUP ~
with Ancho Chilies & Cream

Soup

4 large ears fresh corn, husks and silk removed

1½ tablespoons extra-virgin olive oil

3 shallots, minced

2 garlic cloves, minced

½ celery stalk, chopped

1 carrot, peeled and chopped

¼ small fresh ancho chili, seeded and chopped

2 large tomatoes, peeled, seeded, and chopped (page 163)

½ cup dry white wine

Salt & freshly ground white pepper

5 cups chicken stock (page 159)

¼ cup heavy cream (optional)

Ancho Chilies

1 teaspoon extra-virgin olive oil

¼ small fresh ancho chili, minced

Cream

1 tablespoon sour cream

2 tablespoons heavy cream

Salt

Garnish

Fresh cilantro sprigs

Serves 6

CHEF'S NOTES You can make this dish vegetarian by substituting vegetable stock (page 166) for the chicken stock. Ancho Chili Brioche makes an excellent accompaniment to this soup.

PREPARATION Light a fire in a charcoal grill or preheat a gas grill or a broiler. Grill or broil the corn on the cob until well browned on all sides. Let cool slightly, then cut off the kernels and set aside.

In a soup pot over medium heat, heat the olive oil and sauté the shallots and garlic for about 2 minutes, or until translucent. Add the celery and carrot and sauté for 2 more minutes. Add the corn, chili, and tomatoes and cook for 3 minutes. Add the wine and salt and pepper to taste, and cook to reduce the mixture by half. Add the stock and optional cream, reduce heat, cover, and simmer for 25 minutes.

Meanwhile, cook the chilies and make the cream: in a small sauté pan or skillet over low heat, heat the oil and sauté the chili until tender, 1 to 2 minutes. Set aside. In a small bowl, combine the sour cream, cream, and salt to taste. Refrigerate until serving.

In a blender or food processor, purée the soup until smooth. Strain through a fine-meshed sieve, pressing on the solids with the back of a large spoon to press out the liquid. Taste and adjust the seasoning.

TO SERVE Divide the soup among shallow soup bowls. Using a small spoon, swirl the cream mixture on top of each serving. Garnish the soup with the sautéed chilies and cilantro sprigs and serve.

Imagine lush green rows of trees, laden with gleaming

mangos, oranges, limes. Heady fragrances fill the air;

even the soil smells like fruit. This is Brazil, where some

of the world's finest fruits ripen beneath the tropical sun.

Here the mango's sweetness, the tangy citrus, and the rich,

mild sea bass are wrapped in a banana leaf melding the

contrasting tastes together into one as they cook.

Exuberant Caribbean elements in a dish are complemented by wines with lots of fruit. The Carmen "Special Reserve" **Chardonnay** from the Casablanca Valley in Chile is a perfect accompaniment, showing citrus and fig juiciness to meet the tropical notes of the fish. Another southern hemisphere **Chardonnay** from Rosemount in New South Wales, Australia, displays matching peach and melon notes. The lighter-styled Saintsbury "Garnet" **Pinot Noir** from the Carneros region of California creates a red-berry foil to the rich aspects of the dish, cleansing the palate beautifully.

~ CHILEAN SEA BASS BAKED IN BANANA LEAVES ~
with Glazed Mango & Orange Butter Sauce

Sea Bass

4 banana leaves, each cut into a 9-by-11-inch rectangle

4 Chilean sea bass fillets, about 6 ounces each

Salt & freshly ground white pepper

½ red onion, finely sliced

½ red bell pepper, seeded, deribbed, and julienned

½ green bell pepper, seeded, deribbed, and julienned

4 fresh cilantro sprigs

Orange Butter Sauce

2 shallots, finely sliced

½ cup rice wine vinegar

1 cup fresh orange juice

½ cup chicken stock (page 159)

Leaves from 1 fresh thyme sprig, minced

1 garlic clove, minced

1 teaspoon grated orange zest

1 teaspoon grated lime zest

½ cup (1 stick) unsalted butter, cut into tablespoon-sized pieces

Salt & freshly ground white pepper

Glazed Mango

1 tablespoon unsalted butter

½ teaspoon sugar

1 mango, peeled, cut from the pit in quarters

Garnish

Unsprayed chrysanthemum petals or fresh cilantro sprigs

Serves 4

CHEF'S NOTES   Chilean sea bass is a cold deep water fish with a soft texture and rich flavor. It can be substituted with halibut, turbot, or even salmon. Look for banana leaves in Latino markets. Chrysanthemums are edible flowers with a peppery taste. They may be substituted with cilantro sprigs.

PREPARATION   Begin cooking the sea bass: preheat the oven to 350°F. Warm each banana leaf with a hair dryer to make it more pliable. Sprinkle the sea bass with salt and pepper and place a fillet in the center of each banana leaf. Top with the onion, peppers, and a cilantro sprig. Wrap up in the banana leaf, folding the ends up as if wrapping a package. Place on a baking sheet, folded ends down. Set aside while preparing the sauce and mango.

To make the sauce: combine all the ingredients, except the butter and the salt and pepper, in a small, heavy saucepan. Cook over medium heat to reduce by three fourths. Strain through a fine-meshed sieve into another small saucepan. Return to medium heat and bring to a boil. Reduce heat to a simmer and gradually whisk in the butter one piece at a time. Season with salt and pepper to taste. Set aside and keep warm over a pan of hot water.

To glaze the mango: in a medium nonstick sauté pan or skillet, melt the butter with the sugar over medium heat until the sugar is dissolved. Cook, stirring constantly, until caramelized to a dark brown, 3 to 5 minutes. Cut the mango quarters into fans and sauté, with the fans opened, for about 30 seconds, or until golden on both sides. Set aside and keep warm.

Bake the fish for 8 to 10 minutes, or until opaque throughout.

TO SERVE   Place a packet of fish on each plate. Cut the banana leaf open on top to reveal the fish. Arrange a glazed mango alongside. Drizzle some sauce over each mango. Garnish with the flower petals or cilantro sprigs.

Jambalaya embodies the true meaning of the creole spirit: a blending of cultures and backgrounds that gives life to something completely new. There are countless recipes, brought by slaves from all over the world, but each involves a few key things: zesty local ingredients, an imaginative chef, and a big iron pot for slow-cooking. Our version features smoked ham and spicy Andouille sausage.

This dish has spice and strong savory elements that should be balanced by a wine with fruit intensity. For our cellar selection, the Kenwood "Jack London Vineyard" **Zinfandel** from Sonoma Valley, California, offers spice and plenty of lush berry fruit. The refreshing Domaine Tempier "Classique" **Bandol** (Mourvedre/Grenache/Cinsault) from Provence, France, also has concentrated dark fruit to balance the spice. An equally interesting alternative is the Mulderbosch **Sauvignon Blanc** from Stellenbosch, South Africa, whose juicy tropical fruit flavors and ample acidity create a satisfying equilibrium.

～ CHICKEN JAMBALAYA ～
with Andouille Sausage & Clams

2 tablespoons chicken fat or canola oil

3 chickens, each cut into 8 serving pieces

4 ounces Tasso smoked ham

4 Andouille sausages, sliced

3 large onions, chopped

6 shallots, minced

1 head garlic, minced

2 celery stalks, cut into ¼-by-1-inch strips

2 large red bell peppers, seeded, deribbed, and cut into ¼-by-1-inch strips

2 large green bell peppers, seeded, deribbed, and cut into ¼-by-1-inch strips

2 large leeks, white part only, sliced

1 teaspoon Cajun spice mix

Salt & freshly ground black pepper

1 pound tomatoes, peeled, seeded, and chopped (page 163)

2 cups tomato sauce

1 cup brown veal stock (page 158)

4 cups chicken stock (page 159)

2 bunches green onions, coarsely chopped, including green portions

3 cups Arborio rice

½ cup dry white wine

2 pounds littleneck clams

8 ounces okra, sliced lengthwise

2 bunches cilantro, stemmed and chopped

Serves 8-12

CHEF'S NOTES Andouille hot smoked sausage and Tasso smoked ham are traditional Cajun ingredients which may be substituted with any flavorful alternatives.

PREPARATION Preheat the oven to 350°F. In a heavy ovenproof casserole or cast-iron skillet over medium heat, heat the fat or oil and sauté the chicken until browned on both sides. Using tongs, transfer the chicken to a plate. In the same pan, sauté the Tasso and Andouilles until browned, stirring frequently. Add the onions, shallots, garlic, celery, bell peppers, and leeks and sauté, stirring frequently, for 5 more minutes, or until the onions and shallots are translucent. Return the chicken to the pan. Raise heat to high and cook for 3 minutes. Reduce heat to medium and add the Cajun spices, and salt and pepper to taste. Add the tomatoes and cook for 2 minutes, stirring frequently. Add the tomato sauce and stocks and bring to a boil. Add the green onions and cook for 3 minutes. Add the rice. Stir well and remove from heat.

Cover the pan with a lid or with aluminum foil. Place the pan in the oven and cook for 25 to 30 minutes, or until the rice is tender.

Meanwhile, in a stockpot, bring the white wine to a simmer over medium heat. Add the clams, okra, and salt and pepper to taste. Cover and cook for about 3 minutes, or until the clams have opened. Discard any that do not open. Set aside and keep warm.

TO SERVE Remove the jambalaya from the oven and stir in the clam mixture, combining well. Add the cilantro. Serve in shallow bowls, or bring the casserole or skillet to the table to serve family style.

Jacques Pépin, host of the acclaimed PBS-TV series "Today's Gourmet," is one of the most respected chefs and cooking teachers in America. Adapting traditional French cuisine to the needs of modern, health-conscious cooks, he creates recipes that are stylish, wholesome, and fun to prepare. This succulent broiled lobster is all three — and a highlight of his Guest Chef Dinners on board.

The perfect match for lobster is a full-bodied Chardonnay. From the Santa Ynez Valley in California's Santa Barbara County, our cellar selection is the tropical, mouthfilling Babcock Vineyard "Grand Cuvée" **Chardonnay**. From the same coastline we also suggest the Chalone "Estate" **Chardonnay** from Monterey County, displaying richness with a wonderful mineral character to highlight the pepper notes in the dish. For a richer Chardonnay, the Domaine Gagnard-Delagrange **Bâtard-Montrachet** from Burgundy, France, has a honeyed elegance which embraces the sweetness of the lobster.

~ BROILED LOBSTER WITH BREAD STUFFING ~

A recipe from Jacques Pépin

4 lobsters, preferably female, about 1¼ pounds each

4 slices bread from a large country loaf (8 ounces total), toasted and torn into pieces

2 tablespoons unsalted butter

2 tablespoons virgin olive oil

1 cup minced shallots

8 scallions, finely minced

¼ teaspoon freshly ground black pepper

Tabasco sauce

½ cup dry white wine

Serves 4

CHEF'S NOTES I am very fond of broiled as well as grilled lobster and always prepare it both ways at least a few times every summer. I like to blanch lobsters in boiling water for a few minutes before broiling or grilling. This is the fastest way to kill them, and I find that their meat retains its moistness and is more tender as a result.

PREPARATION Bring a large stockpot of water to a boil. Drop in the lobsters, cover, and cook for about 5 minutes, or until the water returns to a boil. Transfer the lobsters to a plate and let cool to the touch. Reserve the stock for another use.

In a blender or food processor, process the bread to coarse crumbs; you should have 2 cups. In a medium saucepan, melt the butter with the oil over medium heat and sauté the shallots and scallions for 2 minutes. Add the bread crumbs, pepper, and Tabasco to taste, and toss lightly. Remove from heat.

Preheat the broiler. Line a jelly roll pan or the bottom half of a broiler pan with aluminum foil Remove the claws from the lobsters and place them in a heavy plastic bag. Pound the claws with a meat pounder to crack the shells. Transfer the claws to the prepared pan, or remove the claw meat from the shells and transfer the meat to the prepared pan.

Split each lobster in half lengthwise. Remove and discard the stomachs and intestinal tracts. Reserve the juices from the lobster and combine them with the wine in a bowl.

Arrange the lobster halves side by side and flesh-side up on the prepared pan. Lightly fill the body cavities with the stuffing mixture and sprinkle some of the stuffing on the flesh of the tails. Pour the wine mixture around the lobsters.

Place the pan under the broiler on the lowest oven shelf, 10 to 11 inches from the heat source. Broil for about 10 minutes, or until the stuffing is nicely browned and the lobster meat is opaque throughout.

TO SERVE Arrange 2 stuffed lobster halves on each of 4 plates and place 2 lobster claws or the shelled meat of 2 claws alongside. Spoon some pan juices over the lobsters and serve immediately.

This recipe has been reproduced from *Jacques Pépin's Kitchen: Cooking with Claudine*, courtesy of Bay Books, San Francisco ©1996.

Pork is a favorite in the Caribbean, while rich, earthy lentils are popular in France and throughout the Mediterranean. Our chefs celebrate this unique culinary marriage with a blend of spices, vegetables, and creole flavorings, ringed in a zesty citrus-glazed crust as lovely as it is delicious. An example of the creativity that is unleashed when cultures meet!

 The key to pairing wine with a meat dish that exhibits this range of flavors is selecting a wine with intense fruit and without drying tannin or excessive oak. Our cellar selection, the Georges Duboeuf **Fleurie** (Gamay), from the Mâcon region of Beaujolais, France, displays signature black cherry fruit to tame the citrus and the earthy flavors of the lentils. A wonderful, full-bodied alternative from California is the Beringer "Bancroft Ranch" **Merlot** from Howell Mountain in Napa County, California. If a white wine is preferred, a dry, yet very extracted and rich Hugel et Fils "Vendange Tardive" **Riesling** from Alsace, France, amplifies the sweet and sour elements of the dish perfectly.

∼ CITRUS-MARINATED ROAST PORK TOURNEDOS ∼
with Lentil-Vegetable Stew

Marinated Pork

2 teaspoons grated orange zest

1 tablespoon minced fresh thyme

1 teaspoon coarsely ground black pepper

½ teaspoon minced Scotch bonnet chili

2 garlic cloves, minced

2 pounds center-cut boneless pork loin, trimmed

1 cup fresh orange juice

½ cup pineapple juice

2 tablespoons rice wine vinegar

Salt

1 tablespoon vegetable oil

2 tablespoons honey

Sauce

½ cup dry white wine

2 cups brown veal stock (page 158)

1½ tablespoons unsalted butter

Lentil-Vegetable Stew

Stewed Lentils (page 164)

1½ tablespoons unsalted butter

1 small celery stalk, finely diced

1 small turnip, finely diced

1 small carrot, peeled and finely diced

1 large tomato, peeled, seeded, and diced (page 163)

¼ cup minced fresh cilantro

Juice of ½ lemon

1 teaspoon Creole mustard

Salt & freshly ground white pepper

Garnish

1 tablespoon honey

2 tablespoons grated orange zest, blanched (page 158)

4 lemon slices

Serves 4

PREPARATION To cook the pork: in a mortar, grind the zest, thyme, pepper, chili, and garlic to a paste. Rub the paste into the pork and put into a glass baking dish. In a bowl, combine the orange and pineapple juices and the vinegar. Pour this mixture over the pork loin. Cover and refrigerate for 8 hours or overnight, turning once or twice.

Preheat the oven to 375°F. Remove the pork from the marinade and pat dry with paper towels. Sprinkle with salt. In a large, heavy roasting pan or ovenproof skillet over high heat, heat the oil and cook the pork on all sides until browned. Drizzle with 1 tablespoon of the honey. Place in the oven and roast for 10 minutes. Lower the oven temperature to 350°F, turn the pork over, and drizzle with the remaining 1 tablespoon honey. Roast the pork, basting it several times with the pan juices, for about 25 minutes for medium well, or until a thermometer inserted in the pork registers 150°F. Remove the pan from the oven and transfer the pork to a rack set on a sided baking sheet. Cover the pork loosely with aluminum foil and let rest.

To make the sauce: spoon off as much fat as possible from the roasting pan. Place the pan over medium heat, add the wine, and stir to scrape up the browned bits from the bottom of the pan. Continue to cook until the liquid is reduced by three fourths. Add the stock and cook until reduced by two thirds. Strain through a fine-meshed sieve. Pour into a saucepan and bring to a boil. Remove from heat and whisk in the butter. Set aside and keep warm.

To make the lentil stew: drain the stewed lentils, reserving 1 cup of the liquid. In a medium saucepan, melt ½ tablespoon of the butter over medium heat. Add the celery, turnip, and carrot and sauté for 3 minutes. Add the tomato, cilantro, and lemon juice and cook for 2 minutes. Add the remaining 1 tablespoon butter, the reserved lentil juice, and the drained stewed lentils and cook for 3 minutes. Stir in the mustard and season with salt and pepper to taste.

TO SERVE Cut the pork loin into 4 slices. Brush with honey and roll in the orange zest. In a hot oiled grill pan, sear the tournedos on each side for 1 minute. Reserve 4 tablespoons of the stew. Divide the remaining stew among 4 deep plates or shallow soup bowls. Place a tournedo in the center of each serving and top with 1 tablespoonful of the reserved stew. Pool sauce around each serving. Garnish with a lemon slice.

The gauchos are lords of the Argentine pampas, South America's wild west, riding their handsome steeds across the rolling grasslands. In the evenings they gather around an open fire for a meal grilled beneath the stars. This hearty dish of choice grilled steak, roasted vegetables, and spicy red beans captures the rustic, smoky flavors and romantic savor of the free range.

A grilled steak with roasted vegetables calls for the intensity and full body of a substantial red wine. We recommend a spicy, black plum-flavored **Malbec** from Bodegas Weinert in Mendoza, Argentina, a wine that balances the richness of the steak. Another delicious option is the Saxenburg **Cabernet Sauvignon** from Stellenbosch, South Africa, that picks up on the rustic elements of the preparation. Or try the Araujo "Eisele Vineyard" **Cabernet Sauvignon** from the Napa Valley in California, a powerful wine, with a combination of oak and intense dark fruit.

~ GAUCHO-STYLE GRILLED STEAK ~
with Red Bean Chili Sauce & Roasted Vegetables

Roasted Vegetables

3 tablespoons extra-virgin olive oil

⅓ large carrot, peeled, halved lengthwise, and cut into ⅛-inch slices

1 small celery root, peeled, halved
crosswise, and cut into ⅛-inch slices

1 small turnip, peeled, halved crosswise, and cut into ⅛-inch slices

¼ small daikon, halved lengthwise
and cut into ⅛-inch slices

1 onion, halved crosswise and cut into
⅛-inch slices

½ unpeeled small garlic head

½ large red bell pepper, seeded,
deribbed, and cut into 1-inch squares

4 ounces shiitake mushrooms, stemmed
and halved lengthwise

⅛ teaspoon ground cumin

1 fresh thyme sprig

Salt & freshly ground white pepper

1 small zucchini, cut into ⅛-inch
slices

2 tablespoons coarsely chopped fresh
flat-leaf (Italian) parsley

Red Bean Chili Sauce

1 cup dried red beans, soaked in water
to cover overnight

Bouquet garni (page 158)

1 teaspoon extra-virgin olive oil

1 shallot, minced

1 garlic clove, minced

1 small green Anaheim chili, seeded
and diced

½ cup dry red wine

2 cups brown veal stock (page 158)

1 tablespoon unsalted butter

Salt & freshly ground black pepper

Steaks

4 sirloin steaks, about 10 ounces each

Olive oil for brushing

Salt & freshly ground black pepper

Serves 4

CHEF'S NOTES The red bean chili sauce may be made ahead of
time and reheated.

PREPARATION To roast the vegetables: preheat the oven to 300°F.
In a large ovenproof nonstick sauté pan or skillet over high heat, heat
2 tablespoons of the oil and sauté the carrot, celery root, turnip, daikon,
onion, garlic, bell pepper, and mushrooms for about 3 minutes, stirring
constantly. Add the cumin and thyme sprig, and salt and pepper to taste.
Put the pan in the oven and roast the vegetables, uncovered, until tender,
about 25 minutes.

In a small nonstick sauté pan or skillet over medium heat, heat the
remaining 1 tablespoon oil and sauté the zucchini for 2 minutes,
or until lightly browned. Season with salt and pepper to taste. Add
the sautéed zucchini and parsley to the roasted vegetables and mix
together. Set aside and keep warm.

To make the sauce: drain the beans and put them in a medium
saucepan. Add cold water to cover by 2 inches. Add the bouquet
garni, bring the water to a boil, reduce heat to low, cover, and cook
until tender, about 45 minutes.

In a small sauté pan or skillet over medium heat, heat the olive oil and
sauté the shallot, garlic, and diced chili for about 2 minutes. Add the
wine and cook to reduce by three fourths. Set aside.

Drain the cooked red beans and discard the bouquet garni. In a
blender or food processor, combine two thirds of the beans and the
stock. Purée until smooth. Strain the sauce through a fine-meshed sieve
into the red wine mixture. Add the remaining beans and bring the
sauce to a boil. Whisk in the butter. Season with salt and pepper. Set
aside and keep warm.

To cook the steaks: light a fire in a charcoal grill or preheat a gas grill
or a broiler. Brush the steaks with olive oil and sprinkle with salt and
pepper. Grill or broil the steaks for 3 to 4 minutes on each side for
medium rare.

TO SERVE Place a steak on each plate. Serve the vegetables alongside
the steak. Spoon the sauce around the steak and vegetables.

In the brilliant colors and creative textures of this dessert,

our chefs honor the beauty and passion of South America.

The glowing, tender nectarines and bright méringue wafer

suggest the tropical sun, while the unexpected juxtaposition

of tangy fruit and lemon verbena cream with the crunchy

subtlety of hazelnuts has a soulfulness that is vintage

South America.

 A dessert with sweet and tart flavors sings with a wine that shows similar characteristics. Our cellar selection is the Navarro **Late Harvest Gewürztraminer** from the Anderson Valley in California, a wine laced with a hint of lime peel and spice to balance the citrus notes in the dessert. Or consider the off-dry Domaine du Clos Naudin **Vouvray Demi-Sec** (Chenin Blanc) from the Loire Valley of France, a wine that shows fine, apple fruit with balancing acidity.

~ POACHED NECTARINES ~
with Hazelnut Méringue & Vanilla-Verbena Cream

Hazelnut Méringue

2 egg whites

¼ cup confectioners' sugar

3 tablespoons granulated sugar

½ cup hazelnuts, toasted (page 165), skinned (page 164), and finely ground

2 teaspoons flour

Poached Nectarines

4 nectarines, halved, pitted, and each cut into ¼-inch slices

Juice of 1 lime

1 cup dry white wine

1 cup water

½ cup granulated sugar

⅛ teaspoon vanilla extract

Grated zest of 1 lime

Vanilla-Verbena Cream

6 egg yolks

2 tablespoons sugar

2 tablespoons flour

¾ cup milk

1 medium fresh or dried lemon verbena leaf

⅛ teaspoon vanilla extract

Garnish

Confectioners' sugar for dusting

Fresh Bing cherries

Mint sprigs

Serves 4

CHEF'S NOTES Lemon verbena is a potent herb with a strong lemon flavor. It can be found in a farmers' market or a specialty grocery store. Other lemon flavorings such as a blanched strip of lemon zest may be substituted.

PREPARATION To make the méringue: preheat the oven to 400°F. Line a baking sheet with parchment paper. In a large bowl, combine the egg whites, confectioners' sugar, and granulated sugar and beat until soft peaks form. In a small bowl, mix the hazelnuts and flour together. Gradually fold the hazelnut mixture into the egg mixture. Spoon 8 equal rounds of méringue mixture onto the prepared baking sheet. Bake the méringue for 10 to 15 minutes, or until a light golden brown. Remove the pan from the oven and let cool.

To poach the nectarines: toss the nectarine slices with the lime juice. In a small saucepan, combine the wine, water, sugar, vanilla, and lime zest and bring to a boil. Reduce heat to a simmer and cook the syrup for about 10 minutes, or until the sugar is dissolved. Add the nectarines and cook for about 10 minutes, or until tender. Set aside and let cool.

To make the cream: in a medium bowl, whisk the egg yolks with the sugar until thick and light in color. Stir in the flour and enough milk to make a smooth paste. In a small pan, simmer the remaining milk with the lemon verbena for about 10 minutes to infuse the flavor. Remove and discard the lemon verbena. Gradually whisk the milk into the egg mixture. Return the mixture to the pan and whisk over medium heat until it begins to boil. Cook for 2 to 3 minutes, whisking constantly. Remove from heat and stir in the vanilla. Pour the cream into a bowl and rub a piece of butter over the surface to prevent a skin from forming.

TO SERVE Place nectarine slices in the shape of a rosette in the center of each of 4 deep dessert plates. Place 2 tablespoonfuls of verbena cream on top of each of 4 méringue rounds and top them with the remaining rounds. Dust the tops of the méringues with confectioners' sugar and place one on top of each serving of nectarines. Pour the remaining nectarine syrup into each plate. Garnish with cherries and mint sprigs.

This velvety, lusciously rich dessert is a tour de force of South America's most distinctive tropical flavors: bananas hanging in heavy, colorful bunches, the long, purple pods of cacao holding their mellow treasure, and the sweet, resonant perfume of coffee beans growing on steep mountain slopes. On their own, each flavor is delectable; together, they are divine.

Desserts that highlight chocolate cream deserve a wine that is equally sinful and rich. Our cellar selection is the "La Chapelle" **Bonnezeaux** (Chenin Blanc) from France's Château de Fesles in the Loire Valley of France. Its honeyed richness combined with high notes of apricot and spice bring out the fruity notes in the dessert. Another superb combination is found in the luscious orange marmalade flavors of the Quady "Essensia" **Orange Muscat** from the Madera region of California.

∼ CHOCOLATE-BANANA CREAM TART ∼

Chocolate Pastry Crust

1¾ cups all-purpose flour

¼ cup unsweetened cocoa powder

Pinch of salt

1 cup confectioners' sugar

1 egg yolk

1 egg

2 tablespoons water

½ cup (1 stick) cold unsalted butter, cut into small pieces

Filling

¾ cup plus 2¼ cups milk

3 tablespoons cornstarch

5 egg yolks

2 tablespoons unsalted butter

⅔ cup granulated sugar

¼ teaspoon vanilla extract

4 ounces semisweet chocolate, chopped

2 tablespoons banana liqueur or banana flavoring (optional)

Chocolate Ganache

1¼ cups heavy cream

5 ounces semisweet chocolate, chopped

2 bananas, cut into ¼-inch slices

White Chocolate Lattice (page 166)

Garnish

Banana slices

Makes one 9-inch tart, serves 8

CHEF'S NOTES This tart is best when prepared a day in advance and refrigerated. Coffee Crème Anglaise is a nice accompaniment to this dessert. The recipe can be found on page 160.

PREPARATION To make the pastry crust: stir the flour, cocoa, salt, and sugar together in a medium bowl. Stir in the egg yolk, egg, and water until blended. Add the butter and work it into the flour mixture with your fingers until the mixture resembles coarse crumbs. Using a dough scraper or spatula, mix the dough with a cutting motion until smooth.

Turn the dough out on a lightly floured board and, using the heel of one hand, push it away in small portions until all the dough has been smeared. Gather the dough up with a dough scraper or a spatula and press the dough into a ball. Wrap in plastic wrap and refrigerate for at least 30 minutes or up to 3 days.

Preheat the oven to 375°F. On a lightly floured board, roll the dough out to a 13-inch circle. Fit the dough into a 9- or 10-inch tart pan and run the rolling pin across the top of the pan to trim off the dough. Pierce the bottom of the crust all over with a fork. Fit a piece of parchment paper into the crust and fill with dried beans or pie weights. Bake the crust for 15 to 20 minutes, or until lightly browned. Let cool on a wire rack.

To make the filling: in a medium bowl, whisk the ¾ cup milk and the cornstarch together. Whisk in the egg yolks and set aside.

In a small saucepan, combine the 2¼ cups milk, butter, granulated sugar, and vanilla and stir to blend. Bring just to a boil, then reduce heat to a simmer. Gradually whisk about 1 cup of the hot milk mixture into the yolk mixture. Return this to the saucepan and cook, whisking constantly, until thickened, 3 to 5 minutes. Remove from heat and set aside.

In a double boiler over barely simmering water, melt the chocolate. Set the chocolate over a bowl of ice water and stir until cooled. Stir the chocolate into the milk mixture. If you like, stir the banana liqueur into the chocolate filling. Set aside.

To make the ganache: in a small saucepan, bring the cream to a boil. Remove from heat and add the chocolate. Stir until melted and smooth.

Unmold the pastry crust and pour in the filling. Arrange the sliced bananas closely together on top of the filling. Pour or ladle the chocolate ganache over the bananas to cover and glaze the bananas and filling. Prepare the White Chocolate Lattice (page 166), piping the chocolate directly onto the tart. Refrigerate the tart for at least 1 hour.

TO SERVE Cut the tart into 8 slices. Place each on a plate and garnish with 2 banana slices. Serve the Crème Anglaise alongside if desired.

Though one of England's most cherished traditions, bread pudding was always considered a poor man's dish. Then our chefs brought out its inherent promise with the South American magic of coffee and white chocolate, reaching entirely new levels of palate-pleasing intrigue. As the aroma of the first bread pudding filled the kitchen, we knew we had given this favorite dessert a nobility all its own.

 White chocolate is less intense than dark chocolate, allowing for a more fruit-forward wine pairing. Our cellar selection, the Château Rieussec **Sauternes** (Semillon/Sauvignon Blanc) from Bordeaux, France, presents spicy fruit layered with exotic honey and nut flavors that pick up on the sweetness of the pudding. The explosiveness of the **Late Harvest Botrytis Sauvignon Blanc** from Robert Mondavi in Napa Valley, California, displays apricot flavors and rich toasty oak to highlight the coffee notes in this dessert.

～ WHITE CHOCOLATE BREAD PUDDING ～
with Caramelized Coffee Sauce

Bread Pudding

10 ounces brioche or egg bread, crust removed, cut into ½-inch dice (about 8 cups)

4 ounces white chocolate, coarsely chopped

6 eggs

½ cup plus 2 tablespoons sugar

¼ teaspoon salt

1 tablespoon vanilla extract

2½ cups milk

Caramelized Coffee Sauce

½ cup sugar

½ cup heavy cream

3 tablespoons Kahlúa

Garnish

8 scoops Vanilla Ice Cream (page 166)

Chocolate-covered coffee beans

White chocolate curls

Makes 8 individual puddings

CHEF'S NOTES The puddings can be made 1 day in advance, covered, and refrigerated. Reheat before serving. The homemade vanilla ice cream can be replaced by a good-quality commercial ice cream. Kahlúa is a coffee liqueur which can be substituted with strong espresso coffee if desired.

PREPARATION To make the bread pudding: preheat the oven to 325°F. Grease the bottoms and the sides of eight 3½-inch-diameter soufflé dishes with soft butter. Coat the sides and bottoms of the dishes with sugar and tap out the excess. Fill each dish half full with bread cubes. Divide the white chocolate pieces evenly among the dishes. Top with the remaining bread cubes.

In a medium bowl, whisk the eggs, sugar, salt, and vanilla together. Warm the milk and whisk it into the egg mixture until blended. Divide the milk mixture evenly among the dishes. Place the dishes in a baking pan and add hot water to come halfway up the sides of the dishes. Bake the puddings for 45 minutes, or until a toothpick inserted in the center of a pudding comes out clean.

To make the sauce: in a small, heavy saucepan, melt the sugar over low heat, stirring constantly, until golden brown. Remove from heat. Meanwhile, in another saucepan, heat the cream until small bubbles form around the edges of the pan. Gradually whisk the cream into the caramelized sugar. Stir in the Kahlúa.

TO SERVE Drizzle sauce on each plate. Run a knife around the edge of each pudding and invert to unmold. Place a pudding, right-side up, in the center of each plate. Top with ice cream. Garnish with the chocolate-covered coffee beans and white chocolate curls.

Spirit of Adventure

For the early settlers, the American West was a promised land. People flocked there from the four corners of the world, drawn by the fertile soils and teeming waters, and by the freedom of the frontier. They brought the cherished traditions of their homelands, including a dazzling array of foods and cooking styles. Soon the lush plains sprouted unfamiliar herbs, mushrooms, and vegetables, misty river valleys nurtured nut and fruit orchards, a bounty of seafood filled the fishing nets. With a pioneer's eagerness to experiment, cooks adopted the culinary techniques of their foreign neighbors, and tasted the delights of unfamiliar foods — Chinese woks and Latin chilies, sundried tomatoes and cured olives from the Mediterranean. Today these myriad ingredients and ethnic traditions are all part of this region's cuisine, a gourmet frontier whose creativity and innovative use of history are universally respected. Our chefs thrive in this free-thinking

environment, where their inventiveness and broad international experience have free reign. Working with some of the finest ingredients on earth, they create modern classics of world cuisine.

"The American West is a chef's paradise.
New ideas are the tradition,
with some of the world's best ingredients to choose from."
—Toni Neumeister

Alaska's frigid seas, dotted with icebergs and pale blue

glaciers, may seem barren. Yet these chill waters teem with

life, and nourish some of the world's finest seafood. Our

Glacier Cod is line-caught by local fishermen, and selected

by our chefs in ports along the way. Pea shoots and lemon

cream gently complement its delicate aromas; a drizzle of

lobster oil adds a touch of distinction.

A medium-bodied white wine is our recommendation for this delicate fish recipe. A **Pessac-Léognan Blanc** (Sauvignon Blanc/Semillon) from Château Carbonnieux in Bordeaux, France, is our cellar selection, displaying elegance and an earthy accent to the Lobster Oil. A **Sauvignon Blanc** with crispness, the Cakebread from Napa Valley, California, delivers melon and hints of delicious grassiness that build on the pea shoots and citrus. We look to the Arrowood **Chardonnay** from the Sonoma Valley to show a toasty, lemon chiffon quality that mirrors the light creaminess of the sauce.

∼ GLACIER COD ∼

with Pea Shoots in Lemon Cream Sauce & Lobster Oil

Lobster Oil

1 tablespoon lobster stock (page 162)

1 tablespoon extra-virgin olive oil

Salt & freshly ground white pepper

Lemon Cream Sauce

¼ cup heavy cream

¾ cup chicken stock (page 159)

½ stalk lemongrass, halved lengthwise

Salt & freshly ground white pepper

Cod

Four 4-ounce cod fillets

Salt

Pea Shoots

6 cups pea shoots, big stems removed

Garnish

Coarse sea salt

Serves 6

CHEF'S NOTES Cod is a very tender fish and when steamed, it becomes even more delicate. It may be substituted with turbot or halibut. Julienned bok choy or kale may be substituted for the pea shoots.

PREPARATION To make the Lobster Oil: in a small bowl, whisk the stock and olive oil together, with salt and pepper to taste. Set aside.

To make the cream sauce: in a small saucepan, combine the cream, stock, lemongrass, and salt and pepper to taste, and bring to a boil over high heat. Reduce heat to a simmer and cook for 10 to 15 minutes, or until reduced by two thirds. Remove and discard the lemongrass, and strain through a fine sieve into a saucepan. Set the sauce aside and keep warm.

To cook the cod: sprinkle the fillets with salt to taste. Place them in a steamer basket over boiling water; cover and steam for about 4 minutes, or until the fish is opaque throughout.

Meanwhile, in a large pot of boiling water, blanch the pea shoots for about 20 seconds. Drain and add to the lemon cream sauce.

TO SERVE Arrange the creamed pea shoots in the center of each plate. Place a fillet on top of each serving and drizzle the lobster oil around. Sprinkle sea salt over the fish.

California's warm valleys and verdant hillsides are America's produce basket, abounding in fruits and vegetables of every description. From this dazzling palette of colors, shapes, and textures, our chefs have painted a delicious, sunny portrait: the dense meatiness of the portobellos, brightened by fresh greens, plump tomatoes, soft goat cheese, and tangy vinaigrette.

 This is a dish with equal parts sweetness, earthiness, and acidity. It requires a similarly flavored wine, yet one of subtle proportion. Our cellar selection, the **Pinot Noir** from Domaine Drouhin in the Willamette Valley of Oregon, has plentiful cherry fruit to match the sweetness of tomato. It also shows signature earthiness against a silky texture. Similarly, the Luna **Sangiovese** from California's Napa Valley complements the tang of the tomatoes with its crisp red-fruit character. An elegant French Chardonnay, the Louis Latour **Chassagne-Montrachet** from Burgundy, picks up on the earthy notes with its rich mouthfeel.

~ SALAD OF GRILLED PORTOBELLO MUSHROOMS ~
with Sun-Dried Tomato Vinaigrette & Goat Cheese Croutons

Sun-Dried Tomato Vinaigrette

6 oil-packed sun-dried tomatoes, drained and cut into fine julienne

½ shallot, finely chopped

2 tablespoons balsamic vinegar

1 tablespoon Dijon mustard

4 drops chili oil

Salt & freshly ground white pepper

2 tablespoons extra-virgin olive oil

Goat Cheese Croutons

Eight ¼-inch-thick slices French baguette

¼ cup fresh white goat cheese at room temperature

1 teaspoon herbes de Provence

Salt & freshly ground white pepper

Tapenade

8 niçoise olives, pitted and finely chopped

½ tomato, peeled, seeded, and cut into ⅛-inch dice (page 163)

8 oil-packed sun-dried tomatoes, drained and finely diced

Salt & freshly ground white pepper

Portobello Mushrooms

4 portobello mushrooms, stemmed

2 small garlic cloves, minced

¼ cup balsamic vinegar

¼ cup extra-virgin olive oil

Salt & freshly ground black pepper

Salad

8 ounces mixed salad greens

Belgian endive leaves

Salt & freshly ground white pepper

Garnish

Cherry tomatoes, halved

Serves 4

PREPARATION To make the vinaigrette: in a small bowl, combine all the ingredients except the olive oil, adding salt and pepper to taste. Gradually whisk in the olive oil. Taste and adjust the seasoning.

To make the croutons: preheat the broiler and toast the bread slices on both sides until golden, about 1 minute. In a small bowl, mix the goat cheese and herbs together with a fork. Add the salt and pepper to taste. With a small knife, spread the cheese mixture over each crouton.

To make the tapenade: in a small bowl, combine all the ingredients, adding salt and pepper to taste, and blend until smooth. Spread the tapenade on top of the cheese croutons.

To cook the mushrooms: with a small knife, remove the gills underneath each mushroom cap. In a small bowl, combine the garlic, balsamic vinegar, and olive oil. Rub both sides of the mushrooms with the olive oil mixture. Sprinkle the mushrooms with salt and pepper to taste. Let sit at room temperature for about 3 hours.

Preheat the oven to 350°F. Place the mushrooms on a nonstick pan and bake for about 4 minutes.

To make the salad: in a medium bowl, combine the salad greens, endive leaves, and salt and pepper to taste. Toss the greens with most of the vinaigrette, reserving some for later.

TO SERVE Divide the salad among 4 salad plates. Cut each mushroom into a fan and arrange it alongside the salad. Place 2 croutons alongside each salad and garnish with cherry tomatoes. Drizzle the remaining vinaigrette over the salad and mushrooms.

We are honored to serve the exclusive salmon recipe of

Michel Blanchet, former executive chef of L'Hermitage

restaurant in Los Angeles. He smokes prime Atlantic

salmon to perfection, with a unique natural process.

Each element — lemon butter, lightly balanced herbs,

a heart-warming hint of wasabi caviar, the elegant

presentation — makes this the ultimate seafood fantasy.

The Perrier-Jouët "Belle-Époque" Vintage **Champagne**, from France, is our cellar selection for this dish, as the elegant creaminess of the small bubbles provides a perfect contrast to the smokiness of the salmon. A fine alternative is the Roederer Estate **Brut Sparkling Wine** (Méthode Champenoise) from Anderson Valley in Mendocino. Its fruitier, crisp style and effervescence highlights the lemon in the sauce while sweeping the palate clean. If a still wine is desired, we recommend the Far Niente **Chardonnay** from Napa Valley in California, a wine whose richness and vanilla notes bring textural harmony to the dish.

~ TOURTE OF SMOKED SALMON & POTATO ~
with Caviar & Lemon Beurre Blanc

Crêpe Batter

1 egg

Salt & freshly ground white pepper

½ cup all-purpose flour

¾ cup lukewarm milk

2 tablespoons unsalted butter, melted

Lemon Beurre Blanc

¼ cup verjus or Champagne vinegar

¼ cup dry white wine

2 shallots, minced

1 tablespoon heavy cream

1 cup (2 sticks) cold unsalted butter, cut into small pieces

2 teaspoons fresh lemon juice

Salt & freshly ground white pepper

1 tablespoon minced fresh chives

½ tablespoon butter, melted

Smoked Salmon and Potato Tourte

2 tablespoons sour cream

2 tablespoons wasabi caviar

½ recipe hot mashed potatoes (page 162)

8 ounces top-quality smoked salmon, cut into ¼-inch-wide strips

1 tablespoon finely chopped scallion

Freshly ground white pepper

Garnish

4 ounces beluga caviar

1 bunch watercress, stemmed

2 teaspoons fresh lemon juice

Salt & freshly ground white pepper

Makes 8 individual tourtes

CHEF'S NOTES You will need a 2½-inch cookie cutter and a 2½-inch ring mold, available in cookware stores, to make the potato cakes. Wasabi caviar is a whitefish caviar flavored with wasabi (Japanese horseradish). It may be found in Japanese markets and some fish markets.

PREPARATION To make the crêpe batter: in a medium bowl, beat the egg with the salt and pepper to taste. Stir in the flour until smooth, then stir in the milk until smooth. Stir in the melted butter. Strain though a fine-meshed sieve into a small bowl. Cover and let sit at room temperature for 30 minutes.

To make the beurre blanc: in a small saucepan, combine the verjus or Champagne vinegar, wine, and shallots. Bring to a boil, reduce heat, and cook to reduce to about 2 tablespoons. Stir in the cream and remove from heat. Gradually whisk in the cold butter, a few pieces at a time. Add the lemon juice and salt and pepper to taste. Set aside and keep warm over hot water.

To cook the crêpes: brush a 7-inch crêpe pan with some of the ½ tablespoon melted butter and heat over medium heat. Ladle a scant ¼ cup crêpe batter into the pan and tilt the pan to coat the bottom evenly. Cook until browned on the bottom, 60 to 90 seconds. Turn and cook on the second side until browned, about 30 seconds. Put the crêpe on a clean cutting board. Using a 2½-inch cookie cutter, cut out 2 disks. Place on a plate, cover, and keep warm. Repeat 3 times to make a total of 8 circles.

To make the tourte: in a small bowl, combine the sour cream and wasabi caviar. Stir the sour cream mixture into the hot mashed potatoes. Fold in the salmon and scallion, and add pepper to taste.

TO SERVE Oil a 2½-inch-diameter, 1-inch-deep ring mold and place it in the center of a warm plate. Spoon one eighth of the potato mixture into the ring and flatten slightly with the back of a spoon. Remove the ring mold and repeat to make a total of 8 potato cakes. Top each cake with a crêpe round and place 1 teaspoon of caviar in the center. Toss the watercress with the lemon juice, and salt and pepper to taste. Garnish the plates with the watercress. Add the chives to the sauce, spoon around each cake, and serve immediately.

One hot summer day in California, one of our chefs was standing in a strawberry plantation. "The aroma of strawberries surrounded me," he remembers, "so sweet it was intoxicating." In a flash of culinary insight, he imagined capturing this strong, sunny aroma in a luscious soup. The result is the essence of strawberries, with a creamy coolness and a refreshing hint of thyme or mint.

Delicate and refined flavors such as these require a wine that has light body yet enough fruit and sweetness to mirror the dish, not overwhelm it. Our cellar selection is a **Johannisburg Riesling** from Columbia Winery in the Columbia Valley of Washington State. Delectably peachy yet subtle at the same time, this wine shows off the rosy fruitiness of the soup. Equally delicious with this type of summer fare is the Schramsberg **Crémant Sparkling Wine** (Méthode Champenoise) from Napa County in California, a floral, slightly sweet wine that balances as it mirrors the flavors of the berries and cream.

Soup

2 cups fresh strawberries, hulled

1 cup plain nonfat yogurt

2 cups Vanilla Ice Cream (page 166)
or frozen yogurt

Garnish

Thyme blossoms from flowering thyme
sprigs, or mint sprigs

Serves 4

CHEF'S NOTES This soup can be served as either a first course or a dessert. Other fresh berries, such as blueberries, raspberries, or blackberries, can be used in place of the strawberries. The homemade vanilla ice cream can be replaced by a good-quality commercial ice cream or frozen yogurt.

PREPARATION Set aside 2 large, perfect strawberries for garnish. In a blender, combine the remaining strawberries, the yogurt, and ice cream or frozen yogurt and blend until smooth. Refrigerate for about 1 hour.

TO SERVE Julienne the reserved strawberries. Pour the strawberry cream into shallow soup bowls. Garnish with the thyme flowers or mint sprigs and the cut strawberries.

In gourmet cuisine, as in life, it pays to be a perfectionist.

Our chefs spend a whole afternoon hand-picking the finest

Alaskan Dungeness crab from local fishermen. Returning

to the ship, they set to work around three giant soup pots.

Fragrances permeate the air: delicately sweet crabmeat,

aromatic tarragon, redolent tomato. Then we add the Brie,

a touch of robust distinction.

This is the perfect soup for a smoky, medium-bodied dry white wine. Our cellar selection, Peter Michael's "Cuvée Indigène" **Chardonnay**, from Sonoma County, California, offers elegant texture and complex pear-smoke notes to meet the sweetness of the crab head on and counterbalance the richness of the Brie. Another outstanding selection is the Domaine Laroche **Chablis** (Chardonnay) from Burgundy, France, whose unadorned, elegant fruit highlights the licorice flavors of the tarragon. The smoky, rich texture of Robert Mondavi's **Fumé Blanc** (Sauvignon Blanc) from Napa Valley, California, shows a synergy with the richness of this soup as well.

~ ALASKAN CRAB SOUP ~
with Melun Brie Cheese

2 live Dungeness crabs, about
2 pounds each

¼ cup extra-virgin olive oil

1 carrot, peeled and cut into
½-inch dice

1 onion, coarsely chopped

3 shallots, coarsely chopped

1 celery stalk, cut into ½-inch dice

1 small leek, white part only, washed
and cut into 1-inch slices

1 unpeeled head garlic, halved
crosswise

2 tablespoons tomato paste

2 tablespoons flour

2 tablespoons Cognac or brandy

2 cups dry white wine

6 cups water

Stems stripped from 1 bunch tarragon,
leaves reserved

3 large tomatoes, cut into ½-inch dice

Pinch of cayenne pepper

Salt & freshly ground white pepper

½ cup heavy cream (optional)

3 ounces Melun Brie cheese, trimmed
of rind

Serves 4

CHEF'S NOTES Dungeness crab is usually available October through May. It may be substituted with blue crab, king crab, or snow crab. Melun is a particular kind of Brie; other kinds may be substituted if it is not available.

PREPARATION Plunge the live crabs into a large stockpot of boiling water for 2 minutes. Drain and run under cold water to stop the cooking process. Separate the crab claws from each crab. Blanch the crab claws in boiling water for about 2 minutes. Drain and run under cold water. Crack the claws with a hammer or heavy knife and shell them, reserving the shells and meat separately.

Pull off and discard the top shell of each crab. Pull off and discard the breastplate on the bottom of each crab. Remove and discard the gills on either side of the body above the legs, the intestine along the center of the back, and the mouth parts. If you like, reserve the yellowish "crab butter" to use in the soup. Rinse the crab.

Cut each crab in half down the middle, then cut each half into sections with one leg per section. In a stockpot over high heat, heat the olive oil and sauté the crab pieces and reserved claw shells, stirring constantly, for about 3 minutes. Reduce heat to medium and add the carrot, onion, shallots, celery, leek, and garlic. Cook, stirring frequently, for about 6 minutes.

Stir in the tomato paste and flour. Add the Cognac or brandy and white wine. Cook to reduce the liquid by half. Add the water and bring the liquid to a boil. Add the tarragon stems and the tomatoes. Add the cayenne and salt and pepper to taste. Reduce heat to a simmer, cover, and cook for about 30 minutes.

Strain the soup through a coarse-meshed sieve into a bowl, reserving the solids. In another bowl, crush the solids with a pestle or a pounder. Return the strained soup and the crushed solids to the stockpot. Add the optional cream and the crab butter if you like and bring to a boil. Reduce heat to a simmer and cook for about 10 minutes.

Strain the soup through a fine-meshed sieve. Return the soup to the stockpot and bring to a boil, then reduce heat to a simmer. Stir in the Brie. Add the reserved tarragon leaves and claw meat. Cook for about 1 more minute, or until the cheese is completely melted. Taste and adjust the seasoning.

TO SERVE Serve in shallow soup bowls.

Nature has nurtured every colorful ingredient of this dish, creating a medley of vegetables as warm and inviting as a harvest celebration. The fresh asparagus, sweet orange squash, corn, and cauliflower are deepened by the mellow flavors of the mushrooms and enhanced by the mildest hint of spices. This earthy medley is the perfect vegetarian meal.

 The kind of wine that enhances this roasted, earthy vegetable dish is one that has enough round texture and vibrant fruit to elevate its flavors. Our cellar selection is the powerful and complex Patz & Hall **Chardonnay** from Napa Valley, California, with its toasty oak and delicate citrus notes. Another flattering match is found in the strawberry, white pepper flavors of the Château d'Aquéria **Tavel** (Grenache blend) from the Rhône Valley of France. A Bernardus **Sauvignon Blanc** from California's Monterey County is braced by flavors of apple and spice to bring out the green flavors of the asparagus.

~ HARVEST SQUASH ~
with Vegetable Potpourri

Squash

4 serving-sized orange-fleshed winter squash, such as Carnival or Acorn

Vegetable Potpourri

1 large fresh ear yellow corn with husk

2 tablespoons extra-virgin olive oil

½ onion, finely chopped

1 small garlic clove, minced

2 orange-fleshed squash, such as Carnival or acorn, peeled, seeded, and cut into ½-inch dice

2 tablespoons dry white wine

½ cup water

Salt & freshly ground white pepper

4 ounces shiitake mushrooms, stemmed and cut into ½-inch dice

One 3-ounce oyster mushroom, sliced

2 cups cauliflower florets, blanched

12 ounces asparagus, trimmed, blanched, and cut into 1-inch pieces

2 tablespoons heavy cream (optional)

2 tablespoons minced fresh flat-leaf (Italian) parsley

Croutons

1 tablespoon extra-virgin olive oil

1½ cups ½-inch-dice white bread

Garnish

Fresh flat-leaf (Italian) parsley sprigs

Serves 4

CHEF'S NOTES Any other mushrooms, such as portobellos or white mushrooms, may be used in place of the oyster mushrooms and shiitakes.

PREPARATION To make the Vegetable Potpourri: preheat the oven to 350°F. Wrap the squash in aluminum foil. Remove all but the inner layer of the corn husk. Peel back the inner layer of husk and remove all the silk. Smooth the husk back over the corn and dip the ear in water to moisten. Place the squash on a baking sheet and roast for about 20 minutes, then add corn and roast another 20 minutes, or until tender when pierced with a knife.

In a heavy, large saucepan over medium heat, heat 1 tablespoon of the oil and sauté the onion and garlic for about 2 minutes, or until translucent. Add the diced squash and sauté for about 3 minutes. Stir in the wine and cook until the liquid is reduced by half. Add the water and salt and pepper to taste, and simmer until the squash are tender, about 10 minutes. Set aside.

In a large sauté pan or skillet over high heat, heat the remaining 1 tablespoon olive oil and sauté the mushrooms for about 2 minutes, or until lightly browned. Salt and pepper to taste, and add to the squash mixture. Add the cauliflower, asparagus, and optional cream to the squash mixture and cook over low heat for about 2 minutes. Add the parsley. Taste and adjust the seasoning. Set aside and keep warm.

To make the croutons: in a medium sauté pan or skillet, over medium heat, heat the olive oil and sauté the diced bread until lightly golden brown on all sides. Set aside and keep warm.

TO SERVE Remove the husk from the corn. Using a large knife, scrape the roasted kernels from the ear. Remove the foil from the squash. Cut the top 1½ to 2 inches of the squash off (reserve the tops for garnish) and dig out the seeds and strings with a large metal spoon. Add the corn and the croutons to the vegetable mixture and spoon the mixture into the squash. Garnish with parsley sprigs.

This dish unites the delicious cornucopia of Pacific Northwest fish and shellfish. Born in Provence as bouillabaisse, it evolved in nearby fishing villages on the Ligurian coast of Italy as a hearty fish stew which locals called ciuppin. Later it came to America with Italian immigrants, and has taken on a new life as "cioppino," in the cultural melting pot of California.

A dish that evokes so many flavors requires a wine with abundant fruit, and the tomato base requires ample acidity to play an important role. Our cellar selection, a Pinot Noir, fits perfectly: the Francis et Paul Cotat **Sancerre Rouge** (Pinot Noir) from the Loire Valley of France has bright red fruit, slight herbal notes, and acidity to balance the brine of the seafood. The J. Rochioli "Russian River Valley" **Pinot Noir** from Sonoma County, California, plays a similar role, with more black fruit and ripeness. To highlight the herbal character of the dish, we turn to Italy's Villa Antinori **Chianti Classico** (Sangiovese blend), from Tuscany.

~ CIOPPINO ~
with Aioli & Cheese Croutons

Aioli (page 158)

Cheese Croutons (page 159)

Cioppino

3 tablespoons extra-virgin olive oil

1 large onion, finely chopped

2 shallots, minced

4 garlic cloves, minced

½ large carrot, peeled and julienned

1 leek, white part only, washed and julienned

1 celery stalk, peeled and julienned

1 large potato, peeled, halved, and julienned

1 tablespoon tomato paste

1 pound fresh tomatoes, peeled, seeded, and coarsely chopped (page 163)

1 cup coarsely chopped fresh flat-leaf (Italian) parsley

1 cup coarsely chopped fresh basil

4 fresh thyme sprigs

A few saffron threads

Salt & freshly ground black pepper

1 cup dry white wine

2 cups chicken stock (page 159)

2 cups lobster stock (page 162)

12 ounces mussels, scrubbed and debearded

12 ounces littleneck clams, scrubbed

8 ounces each red snapper, and sea bass fillets, skin on, cut into 4 slices

8 ounces halibut fillets, skinned and cut into 4 slices

4 ounces sea scallops

4 ounces medium shrimp, peeled and deveined, with tail

2 to 4 ounces unshelled lobster tail, cut in half lengthwise and deveined

Freshly ground white pepper and cayenne pepper

Serves 4

CHEF'S NOTES The amount of saffron needed depends on the length of the threads and the intensity of the saffron flavor. Adjust the amount accordingly. Chicken and lobster stock enhance the flavor of this recipe but water may be substituted.

PREPARATION Prepare the Aioli (page 158) and Cheese Croutons (page 159) in advance. Then, in a medium stockpot over medium heat, heat the olive oil and sauté the onion, shallots, and garlic for 5 minutes, or until translucent. Add the carrot, leek, celery, and potato and sauté for 3 more minutes. Stir in the tomato paste and tomatoes and cook for 3 more minutes. Add the minced parsley, basil, thyme, and saffron and salt and pepper to taste. Add the wine and cook to reduce the mixture by half. Add the stocks and bring to a boil. Reduce heat to a simmer and cook, uncovered, for about 20 minutes.

Add the mussels and clams to the stockpot, cover, and cook for about 3 minutes, or until the mussels and clams open.

Add the red snapper, sea bass, halibut, scallops, shrimp, and halved lobster tails and simmer, uncovered, very slowly for 4 to 5 minutes. Add white pepper and cayenne to taste.

TO SERVE Serve in shallow soup bowls or in a tureen, accompanied with the aioli and croutons.

The concept of World Cuisine becomes a delicious reality in this innovative blend of ingredients and cooking styles elegantly composed by our chefs. There is tender Alaskan halibut, Japanese miso paste and rice vinegar, French white truffle oil, and Italian olive oil, as well as chanterelles, potatoes, and spinach from the Pacific Northwest. Together they become the best of all possible worlds!

This dish is all about rich notes and brassy earth flavors, calling for a wine that delivers plenty of lush texture. A **Chardonnay** from Robert Talbott in Monterey County, California, is our cellar selection; a wine with a smoky flavor and buttery texture to flatter this complex offering. Or, a highly aromatic, lush **Gewürztraminer** from Domaine Shoffit in Alsace, France, is a stunning partner to the subtle truffle scents and mineral-flavored spinach. For an explosive contrast to the roundness, we recommend the ripe and intensely flavored Petaluma **Chardonnay** from South Australia.

~ BAKED HALIBUT ~

with French-Asian Truffle Sauce, Potatoes Anna & Sautéed Spinach with Chanterelles

Potatoes Anna

1 large russet potato

Salt & freshly ground white pepper

2 tablespoons clarified unsalted butter (page 160)

French-Asian Truffle Sauce

2 tablespoons rice vinegar

½ cup mirin (sweet sake) or sweet sherry

¼ cup sake

½ cup chicken stock (page 159)

1 tablespoon naturally brewed soy sauce

3 drops chili oil

¼ teaspoon red miso paste

¼ teaspoon instant dashi-no-moto

1 cup heavy cream

3 tablespoons unsalted butter

½ teaspoon yuzo or fresh lime juice

¼ teaspoon truffle oil

12 paper-thin slices black truffle (optional)

Salt & freshly ground white pepper

Sautéed Spinach with Chanterelles (page 164)

Halibut

½ tablespoon extra-virgin olive oil

4 halibut fillets, about 6 ounces each

Salt & freshly ground white pepper

Serves 4

CHEF'S NOTES Halibut is a firm, mild-flavored fish. It may be substituted with Chilean sea bass or black cod. Yuzo is bottled Japanese lime juice, available in Japanese markets. It may be substituted with regular lime juice.

Make sure to slice the potato just before cooking to keep it from discoloring. Don't rinse the potato slices or soak them in water, as the potato starch helps to hold the galettes together. The potato is cut with a 1½-inch-diameter coring tool available in kitchenware stores. New potatoes may be substituted for the baking potato if a coring tool is not available.

PREPARATION To make the potatoes: preheat the oven to 300°F. Peel the potato and cut into a long cylinder with the coring tool. Cut the cylinder into 1/16-inch crosswise slices. Divide the potato slices into 4 groups, each with 10 slices. On a baking sheet, place 1 slice of potato as the bottom center and overlap with a circle of 8 slices to form a 3-inch round. Place another slice in the center of the circle as the top center. Repeat to make a total of 4 galettes. Season with salt and pepper to taste.

In a large ovenproof nonstick sauté pan or skillet over medium heat, melt the clarified butter. Using a spatula, transfer the potato rounds to the pan and cook for about 2 minutes, or until lightly browned. Place the pan in the oven and bake for about 5 minutes, or until golden brown.

Remove the pan from the oven and, using a metal spatula, carefully flip the galettes over onto a large plate lined with paper towels. Set aside and keep warm in a low oven.

To make the truffle sauce: in a stockpot, combine the vinegar, mirin or sherry, sake, stock, soy sauce, chili oil, miso, and dashi. Bring to a boil, reduce heat to medium, and simmer to reduce by half, about 10 minutes.

Add the cream and cook to reduce by one third. Transfer to a blender, add the butter, and blend until incorporated. Return to the saucepan. Add the yuzo or lime juice, truffle oil, optional truffle slices, and salt and pepper to taste. Reheat over low heat. Set aside and keep warm.

Prepare the Sautéed Chanterelles and Spinach (page 164).

To cook the halibut: preheat the oven to 375°F. In a nonstick ovenproof sauté pan or skillet over medium heat, heat the olive oil and cook the halibut for about 1 minute on each side, or until lightly browned. Place the pan in the oven and bake for 4 to 6 minutes, or until medium firm to the touch. Season with salt and pepper to taste.

TO SERVE Place the spinach and mushrooms in the center of 4 plates. Place a fillet on top of each serving. Gently place a potato galette on top of each fillet. Spoon the sauce around the spinach and serve immediately.

Our Filet Mignon is a tribute to California's inspired blend of cultures. We started with the quintessential American dish, a superb steak of the finest Black Angus from the Corn Belt, perfectly marbled and aged. We created a unique "steak sauce" by enlivening a classic French rémoulade with the gentle piquancy of horseradish, then added a halo of tangy Middle Eastern hummus, resulting in a thoroughly modern steak.

 The spice and earthy/citrus flavors in this preparation require a wine that has both power and elegance. From our cellar: the Caymus **Cabernet Sauvignon** from the Napa Valley in California, whose black fruit and supple tannins are bold enough for the dish's strong flavors. An equally superb choice for its finesse and subtle earth notes is a Château Lynch-Bages **Pauillac** (Cabernet Sauvignon blend) from Bordeaux, France. The Qupé "Los Olivos Cuvée" (**Syrah/Mourvedre/ Grenache**) from Santa Barbara County, California, offers plenty of rich fruit with subtle smoke character.

Hummus

1½ cups dried chickpeas, soaked
overnight in cold water to cover

1 small carrot, peeled

2 shallots

Bouquet garni (page 158)

1 tablespoon tahini (sesame paste)

2 tablespoons extra-virgin olive oil

Juice of 2 lemons

Salt & freshly ground white pepper

Potato Chips

3 cups vegetable oil for deep-frying

1 large russet potato, peeled and cut
into ¹⁄₁₆-inch-thick slices

Salt

Horseradish Rémoulade

3-inch piece celery, peeled and diced

Pinch of hot paprika

2 tablespoons prepared horseradish

½ tablespoon minced garlic

¾ teaspoon fresh lemon juice

½ tablespoon ketchup

½ tablespoon Dijon mustard

2 teaspoons Worcestershire sauce

¾ teaspoon white wine vinegar

½ beaten egg yolk

Salt & freshly ground white pepper

¼ cup extra-virgin olive oil

Slow-Roasted Tomatoes (page 164)

Filet Mignon

Four 6-ounce filet mignons, preferably
of Angus beef

Salt & freshly ground black pepper

Garnish

Fresh rosemary and oregano sprigs

Serves 4

PREPARATION To make the hummus: drain the chickpeas and put them in a medium saucepan. Add cold water to cover the beans by 4 inches. Add the carrot, shallots, and bouquet garni. Bring the water to a boil, reduce heat to a simmer, cover, and cook for about 2 hours, or until the chickpeas are tender, and drain. Discard the bouquet garni. In a blender or food processor, combine the chickpeas, tahini, olive oil, lemon juice, and salt and pepper to taste, and purée until smooth. Transfer to a bowl and set aside.

To make the potato chips: in a Dutch oven or deep fryer, heat the oil to 375°F. Deep-fry the potato slices for 1 minute, or until golden brown. Using a slotted spoon or a wire-mesh skimmer, transfer to paper towels to drain. Sprinkle with salt to taste. Set aside and keep warm in a low oven.

To make the rémoulade: in a blender or food processor, combine all the ingredients except the oil, using salt and pepper to taste. Blend until smooth. With the machine running, gradually add the oil and blend until smooth. Taste and adjust the seasoning. Set aside.

Prepare the Slow-Roasted Tomatoes (page 164).

To make the filet mignon: light a fire in a charcoal grill or gas grill, or heat a lightly oiled grill pan over high heat. Season the filets with salt and pepper to taste. Grill for 2 to 3 minutes on each side for medium rare.

TO SERVE Pool some hummus in the center of each plate. Place a filet on top of the hummus. Top with potato chips and garnish with the herb sprigs. Serve the tomatoes and rémoulade alongside.

This dish owes its rustic flavors to the golden sun, reflecting the abiding influence of Italian ingredients on California cuisine. The sun ripens the tomatoes to their full tangy flavor, gives the polenta cornmeal its summery yellow hue. Italian immigrants once brought these distinctive foods from the warm Mediterranean, as well as the velvety mascarpone, a unique Crystal touch.

 The sweet and tangy traits of this preparation call for a wine with brilliant flavors and delicate tannins. Our cellar selection, the zesty, cherry-fruited Elio Altare **Dolcetto d'Alba** from northern Italy's Piedmont region, merges perfectly with the tomato flavors. Explosive and earthy at the same time, the Cambria "Julia's Vineyard" **Pinot Noir** from California's Santa Maria Valley is a lovely companion to the dish. California **Chardonnay** lovers will want to explore Meridian's Santa Barbara offering with this dish. The tropical, smoky character enables the fruitiness of the confit to come through.

∼ PAN-ROASTED CHICKEN BREASTS ∼
with Mascarpone Polenta & Sun-Dried Tomato Confit

Chicken

4 chicken breast halves, boned,
with skin on and preferably with
bottom half of wing bone attached
(bones and trimmings reserved),
about 10 ounces each

Salt & freshly ground white pepper

1 tablespoon extra-virgin olive oil

Sauce

Trimmings and bones from chicken
breasts, above, broken into medium pieces

1 onion, cut into 1-inch cubes

1 carrot, peeled and cut into 1-inch cubes

1 celery stalk, peeled and cut into
1-inch cubes

½ unpeeled head garlic

1½-inch fresh rosemary sprig

Salt & freshly ground white pepper

½ cup dry white wine

1½ cups chicken stock (page 159)

2 tablespoons unsalted butter

Mascarpone Polenta

4 tablespoons unsalted butter

2 small garlic cloves, minced

2 shallots, minced

3 cups chicken stock (page 159)

Salt

¾ cup polenta

⅓ cup (3 ounces) mascarpone

2 tablespoons grated Parmesan cheese

Freshly ground white pepper

Sautéed Spinach (page 164)

Sun-Dried Tomato Confit (page 164)

Garnish

Fresh basil sprigs

Serves 4

CHEF'S NOTES Ask your butcher to bone 4 chicken breast halves, leaving the bottom half of the wing bone attached ("Frenching" the wing bone) and reserving the bones and trimmings for the sauce.

PREPARATION To cook the chicken: sprinkle the breasts with salt and pepper to taste. In a large ovenproof nonstick sauté pan or skillet over high heat, heat the olive oil and sauté the breasts, skin-side down, for about 1 minute or until lightly browned; turn and cook on the second side for about 1 minute, or until lightly browned. Transfer the breasts to a plate, reserving the pan with juices for the sauce. Set chicken aside.

To make the sauce: preheat the oven to 400°F. Heat the reserved pan over high heat, add the chicken trimmings and bones, and sauté for about 7 minutes, or until golden brown. Reduce heat to medium and add the onion, carrot, celery, garlic, and rosemary. Cook for about 5 more minutes, or until the vegetables are soft. Season with salt and pepper to taste. Add the wine and stir to scrape up the browned bits from the bottom of the pan. Cook to reduce the liquid by half. Add the stock, bring to a boil, and cook for 5 more minutes.

Place the chicken breasts on top of the sautéed bones, trimmings, and vegetables. Put the pan in the oven and roast the breasts for 5 minutes, or until just opaque throughout. Remove from the oven and transfer the breasts to a plate. Cover them loosely with foil and keep warm.

To finish the sauce, return the pan to the stove. Cook over medium heat to reduce the liquid until ½ cup remains. Add salt and pepper to taste. Strain the sauce through a fine-meshed sieve into a small saucepan. Discard the solids. Bring the sauce to a boil, reduce heat, and whisk the butter into the sauce. Set the sauce aside and keep warm.

To cook the polenta: in a heavy, medium saucepan, melt the butter over medium heat and sauté the garlic and shallots for about 2 minutes, or until translucent. Add the stock and season with salt to taste. Bring to a boil. Lower heat to a simmer and gradually stir the polenta into the stock. Cook, stirring constantly with a wooden spoon, for about 40 minutes.

Meanwhile, prepare the Sautéed Spinach (page 164) and the Sun-Dried Tomato Confit (page 164).

When the polenta is very thick and pulls away from the sides of the pan, add the mascarpone and Parmesan and stir until melted and blended. Season with pepper to taste. Set aside and keep warm.

TO SERVE Spoon some polenta into the center of each plate. Top with spinach and tomato confit. Place a chicken breast on a slight incline on each serving of polenta. Using a soup spoon, pour some sauce around the chicken and the polenta. Garnish each plate with a basil sprig.

Austrian-born Wolfgang Puck is a vital force in the evolution of "California Cuisine." Following the tremendous success of his Spago restaurant, he is also one of America's leading restaurateurs. Chef Puck blends French gourmet training with a virtuoso use of California's varied ethnic styles. This recipe, a favorite of his Guest Chef Dinners when on board, showcases his style: modern, informal, worldly.

 The range of Asian flavors is beautifully highlighted by wines with strong fruit components and supple textural elements. The "Mount Eldelstone" **Shiraz** (Syrah) from Henschke, in the Eden Valley of South Australia, is our cellar choice, offering lush black pepper and black plum notes as a component to the spicy/sweet lamb. Equally dark-fruited, yet with more plushness on the palate, is the Howell Mountain "Black Sears Vineyard" **Zinfandel** from Napa Valley in California. A lighter choice would be a **Côte de Brouilly** (Gamay) from Beaujolais, France, such as the Château Thivin which combines fruit intensity with an easy-drinking quality to stand up to the strong flavors found in this dish.

~ CHINOIS GRILLED LAMB CHOPS WITH CILANTRO-MINT SAUCE ~
A recipe from Wolfgang Puck

Marinated Lamb Chops

1 cup naturally brewed soy sauce

1 cup mirin (sweet sake)

½ cup chopped scallions, including green portions

1 tablespoon red pepper flakes

2 or 3 garlic cloves, minced

12 lamb chops

Salt & freshly ground white pepper

Cilantro-Mint Sauce

1 tablespoon honey

½ teaspoon chopped ginger

¼ cup coarsely chopped fresh mint

¼ cup chopped fresh cilantro

¼ cup chopped fresh flat-leaf (Italian) parsley

½ cup peanut oil

½ cup rice wine vinegar

1 egg yolk

A few drops chili oil

Salt & freshly ground white pepper

Vinaigrette

¼ cup peanut oil

2 tablespoons rice wine vinegar

½ teaspoon red miso

Salt & freshly ground white pepper

1 teaspoon minced fresh ginger

Garnish

8 Belgian endive leaves

12 baby redleaf lettuce leaves

Shredded daikon, carrots, and beets

Fresh cilantro or mint sprigs

Serves 4

CHEF'S NOTES This is my favorite way to prepare lamb chops. The richness of the lamb, combined with the contrasting coolness of the sauce, makes this dish sing in perfect harmony. It goes well with stir-fried vegetables or rice.

PREPARATION Light a fire in a charcoal grill, or plan to sauté the chops on top of the stove. In a glass baking dish, combine all the marinade ingredients, using the salt and pepper to taste. Add the lamb chops and turn to coat. Let sit at room temperature for 30 minutes, turning once.

Meanwhile, make the sauce and the vinaigrette: in a blender or food processor, combine all the sauce ingredients, using the salt and pepper to taste, and purée. Strain through a fine-meshed sieve into a bowl. In a small bowl, whisk all the vinaigrette ingredients together, using the salt and pepper to taste. Taste and adjust the seasoning for each.

To cook the lamb: remove the chops from the marinade. Sprinkle with salt and pepper to taste. Grill over a hot fire for 2 minutes on each side for medium rare. Or, heat an oiled sauté pan or skillet over high heat and cook the chops for 2 minutes on each side; do this in batches if necessary to keep from crowding the chops. Transfer the chops to a platter.

TO SERVE Toss the endive and lettuce leaves with enough vinaigrette to coat them lightly. Pool some sauce on each place. Place the chops on top of the sauce. Arrange the greens to one side, and garnish with the shredded vegetables and the cilantro or mint sprigs.

California is a fruit-grower's paradise, and this lusciously

smooth dessert is a distillation of their freshest tastes

and most intense aromas. These warm, full-bodied citrus

cakes are joined by tart blueberries, tangy lemon zest,

and sweet mangoes, then enveloped in a cool, velvety cloud

of lemon-scented Crème Anglaise — a heavenly chorus

of fruit flavors.

 The strength of this dish — and its obvious connection to wine — is its fruit essence. Our California cellar selection, Bonny Doon's "Vin de Glacière" **Late Harvest Semillon** from the Santa Cruz mountains, meets this dessert with richly flavored fruit and caramelized notes. Dr. H. Thanisch's Bernkasteler Doctor from Germany's Mosel-Saar-Ruwer region offers a cooler climate's rendition of **Riesling Spätlese** with piercing mineral-like fruit and a featherweight body to meet the Mango Sorbet and Lemon Crème Anglaise.

∼ WARM CITRUS CAKE ∼
with Lemon Crème Anglaise & Mango Sorbet

Mango Sorbet

3 mangoes, peeled, cut from the pits, and puréed (2 cups purée)

½ cup granulated sugar

1¼ cups water

¼ cup fresh lemon juice

Citrus Cakes

Butter for greasing the molds

3 eggs

½ cup granulated sugar, plus more for dusting

Grated zest of 2 oranges

Juice of 1 orange

½ cup hazelnuts, toasted (page 165), skinned (page 164), and ground

½ cup all-purpose flour

½ teaspoon baking powder

Pinch of salt

Lemon Crème Anglaise

Finely grated zest of 2 lemons, blanched (page 158)

1½ cups Crème Anglaise (page 160)

Garnish

Candied lemon zest (page 159)

Fresh blueberries

Makes 8 individual cakes

CHEF'S NOTES The texture of this dish is a cross between a moist sponge cake and a soufflé. The distinction of the flavors are enhanced when served warm. Candied zest may be prepared in advance or can be found at specialty food stores.

PREPARATION To make the sorbet: in a blender or food processor, combine all the ingredients and process until blended. Freeze in an ice cream maker according to the manufacturer's instructions.

To make the cakes: preheat the oven to 375°F. Butter the bottoms and sides of eight 3-inch-diameter soufflé molds and dust them with sugar. Tap out the excess sugar.

In a double boiler, whisk the eggs and sugar together. Place over barely simmering water and whisk for about 5 minutes, or until the sugar is completely dissolved and the mixture makes a slowly dissolving ribbon on its surface when the whisk is lifted. Remove from heat and beat until the mixture is room temperature, thick, and pale in color. In a medium bowl, mix the orange zest and juice together. Blend the orange mixture into the egg mixture.

In a small bowl, stir the hazelnuts, flour, baking powder, and salt together. Fold the hazelnut mixture into the egg mixture until well blended. Divide the batter among the prepared soufflé dishes and place them on a sided baking sheet. Bake the cakes for about 35 minutes, or until a toothpick inserted in the center of one comes out clean.

To make the Lemon Crème Anglaise: blend the blanched lemon zest into the Crème Anglaise and set aside.

TO SERVE Run a small knife around the edge of each cake and invert it in the center of a plate to unmold. Place a scoop of sorbet on top of each cake. Spoon the Crème Anglaise around the cakes and garnish with candied lemon zest and blueberries. Serve immediately.

This is one of our most celebrated desserts, a modern version of a classic cheesecake that reveals the creative gifts of our Executive Pastry Chef, Hans Kiendl. One bite sets off a sensual chain reaction of gratifyingly rich chocolate, cream cheese, raspberries... and more chocolate. A masterpiece of the pâtissier's art, which garnered rave reviews at New York's famed James Beard House.

An elegant study in contrasts, our Cheese Tart Moderne fixes the palate on a seesaw between bitter chocolate and red berries and cream cheese. The complex, plum and spice sweetness of Les Clos de Paulilles **Banyuls Rimage** (Grenache) from the Languedoc-Roussillon region of France adds length to the dessert's berry element. Another superb match comes from California's Joseph Phelps **Late Harvest Riesling**. Approachable and lush, its rich texture creates a natural affinity to the cheesecake.

~ WHITE CHOCOLATE CHEESE TART MODERNE ~
with Raspberry Coulis

Chocolate Cookie Crust

Chocolate Cookies (page 159)

3 tablespoons melted butter

Chocolate Tops (circles and cylinders, optional, page 160)

Raspberry Coulis (page 163)

Filling

3½ ounces white chocolate, chopped

2 tablespoons heavy cream

5 ounces cream cheese, at room temperature

3 tablespoons sugar

1 tablespoon vanilla extract

1 egg

1 egg yolk

Garnish

16 chocolate straws

Fresh mint sprigs

Fresh raspberries

Makes 8 individual tarts

CHEF'S NOTES The photograph shows the same presentation of this dessert as when it made its debut at the James Beard House Invitational Dinner. The chocolate tops are technically complicated and difficult to make at home. Some specialty stores may carry chocolate rounds and some configuration of a tower, which may be filled with berries and presented as shown. These tarts are also delicious simply topped with berries and drizzled with the raspberry coulis.

Good-quality commercial chocolate cookies may be used to make the crust if you prefer not to bake your own. The cookie crust may be made 1 week in advance and stored in an airtight container. Chocolate straws may be available at specialty confectionary stores and some candy stores.

PREPARATION To make the crust: finely crush the cookies in a blender; you should have 2 cups crumbs. Pour into a bowl, add 2 tablespoons of the melted butter, and mix thoroughly.

Brush 8 standard muffin cups with the remaining melted butter. Press one eighth of the crust mixture into each cup, forming a ⅛-inch-thick crust on the bottom and all the way up the sides. Place in the freezer until needed.

Prepare the optional Chocolate Tops (page 160) and the Raspberry Coulis (page 163).

To make the filling: preheat the oven to 375°F. In a double boiler, melt the white chocolate with the cream over barely simmering water.

In a medium bowl, beat the cream cheese, sugar, and vanilla together until smooth. Beat in the egg and egg yolk until blended. Blend in the chocolate mixture until thoroughly combined.

Remove the muffin tin from the freezer and fill the 8 crusts equally with the filling. Place the muffin tin in a baking pan and add hot water to come halfway up the sides of the muffin cups. Bake the tarts for 25 minutes, or until the filling is firm to the touch. Set aside and let cool.

TO SERVE Place a tart on each dessert plate. If using tops, place a chocolate circle on top of each tart; place a chocolate cylinder on top of each circle and fill with berries. Pool some coulis alongside each cake. Garnish with chocolate straws and mint sprigs.

This elegant hand-crafted cake is our tribute to

Hollywood, where America lives its dreams. White and

dark chocolate create artistic contours and dramatic

chiaroscuro contrasts, to which luscious chocolate stars

and citrus-sweet Cointreau sauce add a titillating flourish.

Another Oscar-winning performance, by our all-star cast

of pastry chefs.

 The beauty of this dessert is the hazelnut airiness that turns to a rich crumble backed by bitter orange nuances. It calls for a wine which smooths the bitter elements and embraces the sweetness. Marvel at the roasty-caramel flavors of the Far Niente "Dolce" **Late Harvest Sauvignon Blanc/Semillon** from Napa Valley, California, which offers a fruit essence with apricot high notes of its own. For a bright floral, honeyed backdrop to this stunning dessert, sip the Domaine des Baumard, **Quarts de Chaume** (Chenin Blanc) from the Loire Valley of France.

~ HOLLYWOOD CHOCOLATE MOUSSE CAKE ~
with Vanilla-Cointreau Sauce

½ recipe Chocolate Génoise Cake (page 159)

Hazelnut Méringue (page 161)

Orange Confit

2¼ cups water

¾ cup Cointreau

1 cup sugar

Finely julienned zest of 2 oranges, blanched (page 158)

½ cup orange marmalade

Orange Sugar Water

1 tablespoon Cointreau

1 tablespoon corn syrup

2 tablespoons water

Chocolate Cream

11 ounces semisweet chocolate, chopped

2 tablespoons hot water

2 cups heavy cream, whipped

Chocolate Glaze

10 ounces semisweet chocolate, chopped

¼ cup hot water

Vanilla-Cointreau Sauce

2 tablespoons Cointreau

Grated zest of 1 orange, blanched (page 158)

1 cup Crème Anglaise (page 160)

White Chocolate Lattice (optional, page 166)

Garnish

8 dark chocolate stars

8 white chocolate stars

8 orange zest curls, blanched (optional, page 158)

Makes 8 individual cakes

CHEF'S NOTES This is a complex recipe which requires some technical skills. The preparation call for eight 2½-inch-diameter cylindrical molds which are available at most cookware shops. At Crystal Cruises, we make these cakes wrapped in a White Chocolate Lattice; however, for serving at home, this decoration is optional. The chocolate stars and white chocolate coating are available at specialty confectionary stores. Another orange liqueur may be substituted for the Cointreau. Chocolate curls may be substituted for the chocolate stars.

PREPARATION Make the Chocolate Génoise Cake (page 159, cake should be baked in a 9-by-12-inch pan for 25-30 minutes) and the Hazelnut Méringue (page 161) in advance. Blanch the orange zest (page 158).

To make the orange confit: in a small saucepan, combine 2 cups of the water, ½ cup of the liqueur, and the sugar. Bring to a boil, reduce heat to low, and simmer for about 5 minutes, or until the sugar is completely dissolved. Add the chopped blanched zest and cook for about 30 minutes, or until tender. Add the remaining ¼ cup Cointreau, the remaining ¼ cup water, and the marmalade. Bring to a boil, reduce heat to a simmer, and cook for 5 minutes.

To make the sugar water: in a small bowl, combine all the ingredients and set aside.

To make the cream: in a double boiler, melt the chocolate with the hot water over barely simmering water, stirring occasionally. Set aside and let cool. Fold in the whipped cream.

To make the glaze: in a double boiler, melt the chocolate with the hot water over barely simmering water, stirring occasionally. Set aside.

To make the sauce: fold the liqueur and blanched zest into the Crème Anglaise until blended.

ASSEMBLY Lay the méringue on a nonstick baking sheet. Spread the orange confit evenly over the méringue. Lay the génoise cake over the méringue. Sprinkle with the orange sugar water. Spread the cream evenly over the cake. Refrigerate for 1 hour, or until cream is set.

Set the bowl of glaze in a larger bowl of hot water to warm for about 1 minute, stirring constantly with a rubber spatula. Remove the cake from the refrigerator. Using a 2½-inch-diameter cutter, cut 8 rounds from the cake. With a soup spoon, coat the top and sides of each round evenly with the glaze. Refrigerate the rounds for about 15 minutes, or until the glaze is set. Wrap with optional White Chocolate Lattice (page 166).

TO SERVE Place a cake in the center of each plate. Garnish with the chocolate stars on top and the optional blanched orange zest. Spoon some sauce around each cake.

Realms of the Senses From the bustle
and brilliance of a Thai spice market to the silence of a Japanese
rice field to the soul-soothing calm of a South Seas island — each
setting in this vast region is exotic, yet infused with timeless peace.
So it is with the cuisine. From the profusion of colorful ingredients
and ancient culinary traditions, local cooks craft
meals of perfect beauty and order. Moving with
the grace of an artist and the reverence of a Shinto
priest, a Japanese sushi master shapes luscious
seafood into tiny, edible sculptures. Asian chefs
match the cosmic forces in foods, keeping the cool,
mild *yin* of the moon, and the sun's hot, spicy *yang*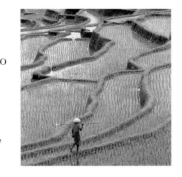
in perfect balance. Art, equilibrium, and a gift for the exotic —
these are the essence of our regional cuisine. The chefs of Crystal
Cruises rejoice in the rare, distinctive foods which they buy in
local markets at every port. Drawing on this region's vast range of
cooking methods and styles, they find subtle harmonies among
the exotic ingredients, creating dishes as beautiful as they are delicious — meals that nourish the spirit as well as the body.

"This is a cuisine of perfect balance, pleasing to the eye as well as the palate.
The unique presentations and flavors can reach elegant, exotic heights."
—Toni Neumeister

Our Kyoto Restaurant features gracefully traditional Japanese cuisine with a Crystal touch, as showcased in this imaginative recipe. We wrap the Tuna Sashimi in nori seaweed and sear it, to seal in its moist richness. The complex tastes of the greens, accented by peppery chrysanthemum petals — an exotic touch of creativity — harmonize perfectly with the vinaigrette's subtle spice.

 Firmly built, intense wines work best with dishes that feature savory flavors. Too much tannin or fruit and the clash will be evident. Tradition calls for a "Daiginjo" **Sake** with true wine-like elegance. Try Horin, from Gekkeikan, which combines mild fruit and steely flavors with a graceful texture. The Yves Cuilleron "La Côte" **Condrieu** (Viognier) from the Rhône Valley of France is a divine selection showing a silken texture and a spicy, powerful frame to stand up to the tuna. An equally delicious pairing is found in the mild fruity flavors and light spicy oak of the King Estate "Reserve" **Pinot Gris** from Oregon's Willamette Valley.

∼ TUNA SASHIMI & WAKAME SEAWEED SALAD ∼
with Spicy Vinaigrette

Spicy Vinaigrette

1 tablespoon sugar

¼ cup rice vinegar

Pinch of salt

1 teaspoon mirin (sweet sake) or sweet
sherry

2 teaspoons naturally brewed soy sauce

1 teaspoon light (untoasted) sesame oil

1 teaspoon chili oil

Pinch of red miso paste

1 teaspoon fresh lemon juice

Wakame Seaweed Salad

2 ounces salted wakame seaweed

1 teaspoon sesame seeds, toasted
(page 165)

1 teaspoon Asian sesame oil

1 teaspoon mirin (sweet sake) or sweet
sherry

1 cup shredded daikon

2 tablespoons fresh unsprayed
chrysanthemum petals (optional)

Tuna Sashimi

1 teaspoon wasabi paste

1 egg yolk beaten with
1 tablespoon water

2 sushi-grade tuna loins, about
6 ounces each

2 sheets roasted nori

1 teaspoon peanut or vegetable oil

Garnish

¼ cup shredded carrot

¼ cup shredded daikon

¼ cup soybean sprouts

Serves 4

CHEF'S NOTES Purchase sashimi-grade tuna loins from a fish market
or a Japanese seafood market. Chrysanthemums are edible flowers
which may be found in specialty food stores. Their petals add a peppery
taste to the salad.

PREPARATION To make the vinaigrette: in a small saucepan,
combine the sugar and rice vinegar. Cook over low heat for about
2 minutes, or until the sugar is dissolved. Add all the remaining vinaigrette ingredients and simmer for about 5 minutes to allow the flavors
to blend. Set aside to cool.

To make the salad: soak the seaweed in water to cover for 30 minutes.
Drain and rinse under cold running water. Squeeze the seaweed with
your hands to remove as much water as possible. In a small bowl,
combine the seaweed and all the remaining salad ingredients and toss.

To sear the tuna: in a small bowl, mix the wasabi and egg and water
mixture together until blended. Brush the tuna loins with the wasabi
mixture. Wrap each tuna loin with the nori seaweed.

In a large nonstick sauté pan or skillet over high heat, heat the oil and
sear the wrapped tuna loins on all sides for about 1 minute. Transfer to
a plate to rest for 2 minutes. Cut each loin into 20 equal pieces about
³⁄₈ inch thick.

TO SERVE Place the seaweed salad in the center of plates with rims.
Arrange 5 slices of tuna sashimi on top of each serving of salad.
Garnish with the carrot, daikon, and soybean sprouts, with the vinai-
grette on the side.

Wontons are a Chinese institution: tender, delectable morsels tucked away in their little packets of dough, a mystery to the uninitiated. Our version of this Asian classic has nothing to hide. A tempting blend of Chinese spices, nuts, and tender chicken sits proudly in crispy open cups of wonton, offering up the flavors of the East with a stylish Western presentation.

We suggest a wine that has texture and aromatic fruit in equal measure to this quintessential Chinese dish. Our cellar selection is just that: the melon, pineapple flavors of Orlando "Jacob's Creek" **Semillon/ Chardonnay** from Southern Australia, provide a perfect foil to the richer aspects while keeping the pepper and sweet flavors in check. A similar blend is Château Margaux's **Pavillon Blanc** (Sauvignon Blanc/Semillon) of Bordeaux, France. For a fruitier alternative, Fetzer's Mendocino County **Gewürztraminer** from California has spicy aromas and lightly sweet peach flavor.

~ MANDARIN MINCED CHESTNUT CHICKEN ~
in Wonton Cups

Wonton Cups

4 cups vegetable oil for deep-frying

Four 4-inch-square wonton wrappers

Seasoning Sauce

2 teaspoons naturally brewed soy sauce

1 teaspoon mirin (sweet sake) or sweet sherry

½ teaspoon chili sauce, preferably sriracha (available in Asian markets)

½ teaspoon hoisin sauce

Freshly ground white pepper

Chestnut Chicken

½ egg white, lightly beaten

½ tablespoon cornstarch

½ tablespoon Asian sesame oil

Salt & freshly ground white pepper

3 ½ ounces skinless boneless chicken breast meat, finely diced

2 tablespoons vegetable oil

1 teaspoon minced shallot

½ teaspoon minced garlic

2 tablespoons finely diced water chestnuts

1 tablespoon finely diced red bell pepper

1 ½ tablespoons finely diced snow peas

Garnish

½ cup shredded iceberg lettuce

½ tablespoon roasted peanuts, finely chopped

Serves 4

PREPARATION To make the wonton cups: in a small skillet over high heat, heat the oil to 375°F. Add 1 wonton square and, using a small ladle, push the square down into the oil while cooking it until golden brown, about 1 minute. The wonton sheet will take on the round shape of the ladle as it cooks. Using a slotted spoon or a wire-meshed skimmer, transfer the cup to paper towels to drain. Repeat three times to cook the remaining squares.

To make the sauce: in a small bowl, stir all the ingredients together, using the pepper to taste. Set aside.

To cook the chicken: in a medium bowl, mix the egg white, cornstarch, and sesame oil together. Season with salt and pepper to taste. Toss the chicken with the egg white mixture to coat evenly. In a small saucepan of salted boiling water, blanch the chicken for about 30 seconds, or until opaque.

In a wok or in a large nonstick skillet over high heat, heat the oil and stir-fry the shallot and garlic for 10 seconds. Add the water chestnuts, bell pepper, and snow peas and stir-fry for 10 more seconds. Add the chicken and stir-fry for 20 seconds.

Add the seasoning sauce to the chicken and stir-fry for 10 seconds. Remove from heat. Taste and adjust the seasoning. Set aside and keep warm.

TO SERVE Divide the lettuce among the 4 wonton cups. Divide the chestnut chicken among the cups and sprinkle each serving with peanuts. Serve immediately

Yin and yang expresses the harmonious interplay of

opposites, a fundamental tenet of Chinese philosophy.

This beautiful equilibrium is also the key to our Lobster

Dumplings, whose dense flavors are enlivened by two

opposing sauces: the cool green sweetness of the Yin sauce,

perfectly balanced with the sunny orange spice of the Yang.

Cosmic harmony becomes a delicious reality.

 When rich lobster comes wrapped in tang and spice, there are few better wines to meet it than our cellar choice, a silky yet mouth-wateringly racy Hunters **Sauvignon Blanc** from New Zealand's Marlborough region. For an aromatic alternative, Alban Vineyards **Viognier**, from the Edna Valley of San Luis Obispo, stands up to the distinction of both sauces with its own spice and ripe fruit. Another fine option is also found in the Chateau Ste. Michele **Johannisberg Riesling** from Columbia Valley in Washington, crisp and well proportioned with peach and apple flavors.

~ FRIED LOBSTER DUMPLINGS ~
with Yin-Yang Sauces

Yin Sauce

1 tablespoon sugar

3 tablespoons rice vinegar

2 kiwifruits, peeled and puréed

½ teaspoon wasabi paste

Yang Sauce

1 tablespoon sugar

¼ cup rice vinegar

1 carrot, peeled, cooked, and puréed

Pinch of cayenne pepper

Lobster Dumplings

6 ounces raw lobster tail meat, finely diced

⅓ cup finely chopped scallion, including green portions

½ teaspoon minced fresh ginger

Salt & freshly ground white pepper

1 teaspoon cornstarch

¼ cup water

Twelve 4-inch-square wonton wrappers

3 cups vegetable oil for deep-frying

Serves 4

PREPARATION To make the Yin Sauce: in a small saucepan, combine the sugar and rice vinegar and cook over low heat, stirring, until the sugar is dissolved. Let cool. Add the kiwi purée and wasabi. Set aside.

To make the Yang Sauce: in a small saucepan, combine the sugar and rice vinegar and cook over low heat, stirring, until the sugar is dissolved. Let cool. Add the carrot purée and cayenne. Set aside.

To make the dumplings: in a small bowl, combine the lobster, scallion, ginger, and salt and pepper to taste. In a cup, mix the cornstarch and water together. Lay the wonton squares out on a work surface and brush the edges of each one with some of the cornstarch mixture. Place 1 tablespoon filling in the center of each square. Gather up the edges to make a bag. Lift the bag onto your hand and squeeze it gently above the filling as if to make a neck on the bag. While holding the neck, press down on the filling to create a little sack. Repeat to form the remaining dumplings.

In a Dutch oven or deep fryer, heat the oil to 375°F. Add the dumplings in two batches and fry until golden brown, about 20 seconds. Using a slotted spoon or wire-mesh skimmer, transfer to paper towels to drain.

TO SERVE Arrange 3 dumplings on each plate and serve with the sauces on the side.

In Japanese myth, miso is a gift from the gods, the Asian counterpart to manna from heaven. These simple soups flavored with thick, fermented soybean paste are essential to daily Japanese cuisine. Our Japanese chefs respect the ageless tradition of miso, adding each ingredient with painstaking care, serving each bowl with reverence and pride: bringing our guests a little bit of Asian serenity.

This delicious soup is rich with the meaty, yet fresh flavors of the red soy bean from which it is derived. Traditionally it is enjoyed throughout the meal as a palate refresher to prepare you for the next course and therefore is not paired with wine.

1½ ounces wakame seaweed

4½ cups water

½ cup red miso paste

*⅓ cup finely chopped scallion,
including green portion*

4 ounces tofu, cut into ¼-inch dice

*2 ounces shiitake mushrooms, stemmed
and coarsely sliced*

Serves 6

PREPARATION Soak the seaweed in water to cover for 30 minutes. Drain and rinse under cold running water, and squeeze the seaweed with your hands to remove as much water as possible. Cut the seaweed into pieces about 1 by 1½ inches.

In a medium saucepan, combine the water and miso paste and bring to a boil. Reduce heat to low and simmer for about 5 minutes. Add the seaweed and scallion. Just before serving, add the tofu and shiitakes.

TO SERVE Serve in Japanese bowls with lids.

In every Asian port of call, our chefs visit country markets in search of rare local ingredients, which give our Asian cuisine its authentic savor. In Thailand, they might return to the ship with citrus-flavored kaffir lime leaves and lemongrass; a local ginger called galangal; and nam pla, a prized thick, salty fish sauce. These exotic materials form the basis of our hot and sour soup.

 The contrasting notes in this dish require a wine that has enough gusto to meet the citrus and spice, and enough textural depth to handle the rich coconut. The Lindemans "Padthaway" **Chardonnay** from South Australia, shows richness with great fruit depth, making it a good selection for a soup with this level of intensity. A wine that picks up on the high citrus and spice notes in the soup is the Navarro **Gewürztraminer** from California's Anderson Valley. Aromatic and crisp, it mirrors the lime leaf and lemongrass beautifully.

~ THAI CHICKEN & SHRIMP SOUP ~
with Galangal & Lemongrass

4 cups chicken stock (page 159)

8 fresh or frozen kaffir lime leaves

12 paper-thin slices galangal
(Thai ginger)

1 stalk lemongrass, white part only, cut
crosswise into 4 slices (leaves reserved
for garnish)

4 dried Thai chilies, or 1 fresh Thai
chili, seeded and minced

4 ounces boneless, skinless chicken
thigh meat, cut into thin strips

2 ounces assorted mushrooms, such as
white, oyster, and stemmed shiitakes,
coarsely sliced

1 tablespoon Thai fish sauce (nam pla)

½ cup coconut milk

4 large shrimp in the shell

4 sea scallops (optional)

Juice of 1 lime

1 scallion, finely sliced, including
green portion

¼ cup chopped fresh cilantro

Garnish

Reserved lemongrass leaves

Fresh Cilantro sprigs

Fresh or dried Thai chilies, halved
lengthwise

Serves 4

CHEF'S NOTES Look for kaffir lime leaves and galangal (Thai ginger) in Asian markets. Any fresh ginger may be substituted for the galangal.

PREPARATION In a soup pot, bring the stock to a simmer over medium heat. Add the lime leaves, galangal, lemongrass, chilies or chili, and chicken. Reduce heat to low and cook for about 10 minutes. Add the mushrooms and cook for 3 to 4 minutes. Add the fish sauce and coconut milk. Bring the soup to a boil again and cook for about 2 minutes. Reduce heat to low, add the shrimp and optional scallops, and cook for about 3 minutes, or until the shrimp are pink and the scallops are opaque.

Remove from heat and add the lime juice, scallion, and cilantro. Let sit for about 5 minutes for the flavors to mingle.

TO SERVE Ladle into deep bowls or cups, garnished with lemongrass leaves, cilantro sprigs, and chilies.

Chinese scholar, award-winning cooking instructor, and author of the classic American texts on Chinese cuisine, Barbara Tropp is an ambassador of modern Chinese cooking in America. She has featured this dish during her Guest Chef Dinners on board: casual but impeccably balanced, a marriage of traditional Chinese tastes and cooking techniques with a contemporary flair that has made her famous.

Duck's natural partner in the wine world is undoubtedly **Pinot Noir**. Our cellar selection, the Cooper Mountain Vineyards "Reserve" from the Willamette Valley of Oregon, delivers spice and bright red fruit to cut the duck's strong oily character. There are other fine options that play off the sharp ginger, such as the complex, powerful "Goldert Clos St. Imer" Grand Cru **Tokay-Pinot Gris** from Ernest Burn of Alsace, France. Or, to highlight the tangy flavors of the marinade with exuberant lychee fruit and spice, we look to British Columbia's Okanagan Valley for the Sumac Ridge "Private Reserve" **Gewürztraminer**.

A recipe from Barbara Tropp

Ginger Oil

¼ cup very finely julienned
fresh ginger

1¼ cups corn, peanut, or canola oil

Marinade

¼ cup naturally brewed soy sauce

2 tablespoons mushroom soy sauce

¼ cup Chinese rice wine or dry sherry

1 tablespoon ginger oil, above

2 teaspoons sugar

1 scallion, cut into 1-inch lengths and
crushed

3 quarter-sized coins fresh ginger,
crushed

1 tablespoon finely slivered cilantro
sprigs with stems

Duck

4 fresh individual duck breasts, skinned
and trimmed

2 tablespoons or more ginger oil, above

Vinaigrette

2 tablespoons fresh ginger juice,
squeezed from finely minced fresh ginger

Finely grated zest of 1 to 2
well-scrubbed oranges

1 tablespoon balsamic vinegar

½ teaspoon naturally brewed soy sauce

¼ teaspoon kosher salt

Several twists freshly ground pepper

1 to 2 tablespoons fresh orange juice,
sweetened to taste

½ cup ginger oil, above

Salad

10 cups mixed baby salad greens

¼ cup sliced almonds, toasted
(page 165)

Serves 4

CHEF'S NOTES The garnish of crispy ginger threads is unique. The frying oil, flavored from the ginger, is then used for marinating and searing the duck. If there is a bit left over, refrigerate it for stir-frying or salad-making. An extra ginger note comes from the splash of fresh squeezed ginger juice in the vinaigrette. You will need more or less ginger to start depending on the juiciness of the ginger. For a special touch, sear the duck shortly before serving to enjoy the contrast of warm meat and cool greens. Fruit makes a wonderful addition to the salad: slices of sweet orange, slivers of crisp Asian apple, or clusters of tiny Champagne grapes tucked in or set alongside are all delicious.

PREPARATION To make the ginger oil: in a wok or heavy skillet over medium heat, heat the oil to 375°F, or until a thread of ginger bubbles when dropped into the oil. Turn off the heat. Add the ginger, swish the threads gently apart with chopsticks, and cook until they turn light golden, about 10 seconds. Immediately strain the oil through a fine-meshed sieve set over a heatproof bowl. Scatter the ginger on a plate lined with paper towels. Reserve the oil.

To make the marinade: in a glass baking dish just big enough to hold the duck breasts in one layer, mix all the ingredients together. Add the duck breasts and turn to coat. Let sit at room temperature for 1 hour, turning the breasts over after 30 minutes.

To cook the duck: preheat the oven to 400°F. Drain the duck breasts and discard the marinade. Heat a wok or large heavy skillet over high heat until a bead of water evaporates on contact. Add 2 tablespoons ginger oil, and swirl to glaze the pan. Add the duck breasts in a single layer (cook them in 2 batches if necessary). Sear for about 2 minutes, or until a deep golden brown on the bottom. Turn and sear on the second side until brown, about 1 minute, adding more oil if necessary to prevent sticking.

Put the seared duck breasts side by side on a rack set over a baking sheet. Place in the oven and roast for about 4 minutes, or until medium rare; check by cutting into the thickest portion of the breast to see if the duck is done to your liking. Remove from the oven.

To make the vinaigrette: whisk the ginger juice, orange zest, vinegar, soy sauce, salt, pepper, and orange juice until blended. Add the ginger oil in a thin stream, whisking to emulsify. Taste and adjust seasoning to your liking. Leave the whisk alongside the bowl.

TO SERVE Cut the duck on the diagonal into thin ribbons. Fan the duck attractively along the rim of 4 serving plates. Re-whisk the vinaigrette to emulsify. In a large bowl, toss the greens and toasted almonds with enough vinaigrette to coat lightly. Mound the salad in the center of the plates and garnish with a sprinkling of the crispy ginger threads. Drizzle a bit of the vinaigrette over the duck to glaze it.

Gentle tradewinds rustle in the palms, ruffling the surface of a glassy lagoon. The serenity of the South Pacific inspired this elegant dish, and its azure waters nurtured the opah, a prized local fish. Against the resonant fullness of its sweet, pink flesh, other tastes emerge like stars in the evening sky: pecans and sesame, delicately bitter bok choy, and sweetly sour apple cider.

Delicate, sweet fish with subtle textures requires a wine that has depth without overtly fruity character or excessive tannins. Our cellar selection, the Kumeu River **Chardonnay** from the Kumeu region of New Zealand, has richness to harmonize with the complex flavors and textures of the sauce. A wholly different, but complementary style is the Gravner **Chardonnay** from Friuli, Italy, which creates a steely foil to the dish, elevating the cider notes. The Ponzi "Reserve" **Pinot Noir** from the Willamette Valley of Oregon maintains elegant cherry flavors that mesh with the sweetness of the fish.

~ SESAME-CRUSTED OPAH ~
with Wok-Fried Bok Choy, Eggplant & Apple Cider Sauce

Apple Cider Sauce

2 cups apple cider wine

1 cup apple cider vinegar

1 tablespoon naturally brewed soy sauce

6 tablespoons unsalted butter, cut into ½-inch dice

Salt & freshly ground white pepper

Opah

4 opah fillets, about 6 ounces each

Salt & freshly ground white pepper

2 tablespoons white sesame seeds

2 tablespoons black sesame seeds

1 egg white

1 tablespoon peanut oil

Wok-Fried Bok Choy

4 ounces bok choy, coarsely chopped

1 tablespoon vegetable oil

2 shallots, finely sliced

1 teaspoon naturally brewed soy sauce

Salt & freshly ground white pepper

Eggplant

1 tablespoon extra-virgin olive oil

1 Japanese eggplant, cut into 20 thin diagonal slices

Salt & freshly ground white pepper

Garnish

Honeyed Pecan Halves (page 161)

Fresh savory or cilantro sprigs

Serves 4

CHEF'S NOTES Opah is a Hawaiian fish with firm pink flesh. It is also known as moonfish. Mahimahi, tuna, or red snapper may be substituted.

PREPARATION To make the sauce: in a small, heavy saucepan, combine the wine and vinegar. Cook over low heat to reduce the liquid by two thirds. In a blender, combine the wine mixture and soy sauce. With the machine running, add the butter one piece at a time and blend until smooth. Season with salt and pepper to taste. Set aside and keep warm over hot water.

To cook the opah: preheat the oven to 375°F. Season the fillets with salt and pepper. Mix the sesame seeds and spread on a plate. Brush one side of each fillet with the egg white and dip in the sesame seed mixture to coat.

In a large ovenproof nonstick sauté pan or skillet over medium heat, heat the peanut oil and cook the fish, coated-side down, for 1 minute, then turn and cook on the second side for 1 minute. Put the pan in the oven and roast the fish for 5 more minutes, or until medium-firm to the touch. Remove the pan from the oven, set it aside, and cover the pan to keep the fillets warm.

To cook the bok choy: blanch the bok choy in boiling water for about 30 seconds. Using a wire-mesh skimmer, transfer to ice water, then to paper towels to drain. In a wok or a medium nonstick skillet over high heat, heat the oil and sauté the shallots for about 30 seconds, or until golden brown. Add the bok choy and soy sauce, and the salt and pepper to taste. Stir-fry for a few seconds to heat. Set aside and keep warm.

To cook the eggplant: in a medium nonstick skillet over medium heat, heat the oil and sauté the eggplant slices for 1 minute, or until golden brown on both sides. Using a slotted spoon, transfer to paper towels to drain. Season with salt and pepper to taste.

TO SERVE Place a fillet in the center of each plate, crust-side up. Pour some sauce around each fillet. Arrange some bok choy and eggplant around the fish. Garnish with pecans and herb sprigs.

Teppanyaki simply means "iron grill," yet the Japanese eye for creative presentation can turn basic cooking into a work of art. Here a gathering of grilled, lightly spiced lobster tail, scallops, and mushrooms sits in a miniature boat fashioned from kombu seaweed, sailing the gentle seas of your plate. The dish becomes a gracious, poetic gift, from our Japanese chefs to our guests.

 The purity of flavors in much of Japan's cuisine calls for a wine that has graceful structure. The F-X Pichler, Von den Terrassen **Grüner Veltliner Smaragd** from the Loibnerberg region of Wachau, Austria, is our choice for this selection, with restrained pineapple and almond elements that complement the subtlety found here. Two **Chardonnays** come to mind to highlight the richer aspects: the Newton from Napa Valley, California, and the Pierro from the Margaret River in Australia. Both have silkiness and fig-like complexity to carry the textural elements of the dish.

~ SEAFOOD TEPPANYAKI ~
with Shiitake Mushrooms in Fried Kombu Boats

Fried Kombu Boats

4 kombu leaves, cut into 6-by-4-inch pieces

3 cups vegetable oil for deep-frying

Teppanyaki

1 tablespoon vegetable oil

12 ounces raw lobster tail meat, cut into ½-inch slices

12 sea scallops

2 ounces small white mushrooms

2 garlic cloves, sliced

2 scallions, green part only, cut into 1-inch pieces

1 tablespoon naturally brewed soy sauce

1 tablespoon mirin (sweet sake) or sweet sherry

4 tablespoons unsalted butter

Freshly ground white pepper

Garnishes

Lobster tail shells

Small pine branches

Lemon wedges

Serves 4

CHEF'S NOTES Our Teppanyaki is made with seafood but it may also be prepared with poultry, meat, or vegetables. A heavy iron skillet is the best substitute for the traditional Teppanyaki grill, however, a standard nonstick sauté pan may also be used. Kombu is a dried seaweed available in Asian markets and some supermarkets.

PREPARATION To make the Kombu Boats: cut 2 long thin strips from each kombu leaf to use as a string. Gather each end of each leaf together and tie with a kombu strip to form a boat shape.

In a Dutch oven or deep skillet, heat the oil to 375°F. Add the kombu boats and deep-fry for about 1 minute, or until crisp. Using a slotted spoon or a wire-mesh skimmer, transfer to paper towels to drain.

To make the Teppanyake: in a heavy iron skillet or large nonstick sauté pan over high heat, heat the oil and sauté the lobster and scallops for about 1 minute, or until the lobster is opaque and the scallops are lightly browned. Add the mushrooms, garlic, and scallions and sauté for 1 minute. Stir in the soy sauce and mirin or sherry and cook to reduce the liquid by one third. Stir in the butter and season to taste with pepper. The lobster and scallops should now be opaque throughout.

TO SERVE Divide the Teppanyake among the Kombu Boats. Garnish as desired.

The lotus blossom is a recurrent image in Asia, its delicate petals around the central flower symbolizing the beauty and complexity of life. The presentation of this dish mimics the lotus blossom's graceful shape, with petals of lightly seared beef tenderloin set around an ornate nest of crispy fried spinach, wonton, and julienned vegetables, in a citrus-spicy sauce.

Dueling flavors of soy and citrus overlaying red meat demand a wine with striking fruit. Our cellar selection, the Rockford Dry Country **Grenache** from Barossa Valley, South Australia, underscores this balancing act with spicy aromas and robust red fruit. Other rich, dark-fruited wine options include the Simi "Reserve" **Cabernet Sauvignon** from California's Alexander Valley, and the Château Magdelaine **St. Emilion** (Merlot/Cabernet Sauvignon) from the Bordeaux region of France. Both offer plenty of fruit intensity and structure to stand up to the strong flavors accompanying the beef.

~ SEARED BEEF TENDERLOIN SLICES ~
with Fried Spinach & Kaffir Lime-Shallot Sauce

Kaffir Lime-Shallot Sauce

2 tablespoons vegetable oil

¼ cup minced shallots

½ teaspoon red pepper flakes

2 kaffir lime leaves, finely julienned

Pinch of ground cumin

Pinch of ground coriander

3 tablespoons light soy sauce

3 tablespoons sweet Chinese chili sauce

2 tablespoons rice wine vinegar

½ tomato, peeled, seeded, and chopped
(page 163)

½ tablespoon tomato paste

2 tablespoons roasted peanuts, ground

Marinated Beef

2 tablespoons light soy sauce

2 tablespoons sweet Chinese chili sauce

2 teaspoons grated fresh ginger

12 ounces beef tenderloin, cut into
¼-inch-thick slices

Fried Wonton Strips and Spinach

2 cups vegetable oil for deep-frying

Eight 4-inch-square wonton wrappers,
cut into ¼-inch-wide strips

2 cups baby spinach leaves

2 tablespoons vegetable oil for cooking
the beef

Garnish

½ cup finely julienned carrot

½ cup finely julienned red bell pepper

1 cup finely julienned daikon

Thin lime slices

Fresh kaffir lime leaves or cilantro sprigs

Serves 4

CHEF'S NOTES To simplify this dish, delete the fried spinach.

PREPARATION To make the sauce: in a small, heavy saucepan, over low heat, heat the oil and sauté the shallots and pepper flakes for about 2 minutes. Add all the remaining sauce ingredients. Bring to a boil, reduce heat, and simmer the sauce for 15 minutes. Set aside.

To marinate the beef: in a small bowl, combine all the marinade ingredients. Add the tenderloin slices, stir to coat, and marinate at room temperature for about 10 minutes.

To fry the wonton strips and spinach: in a Dutch oven or deep fryer, heat the vegetable oil to 375°F. Fry the wonton strips for 15 seconds, or until golden brown. Using a slotted spoon or a wire-mesh skimmer, transfer to paper towels to drain. In the same oil, fry the spinach leaves for about 10 seconds, or until nicely crisp. Using a slotted spoon or a wire-mesh skimmer, transfer to paper towels to drain.

To cook the beef: in a wok or a large nonstick sauté pan or skillet over high heat, heat the oil and stir-fry the beef tenderloin slices on all sides for about 15 seconds. Add the sauce and stir to coat the slices. Remove from heat.

TO SERVE Arrange the beef tenderloin slices on the plates. Top with the wonton strips and spinach leaves. Garnish with julienned vegetables, lime slices, and lime leaves or cilantro sprigs.

When the diverse ingredients and culinary traditions of the Orient come together in one dish, exciting new synergies can emerge. Here the pale, firm Opakapaka from Hawaii dons a resplendent gown of Japanese shiitake mushrooms and Thai lemongrass, and is bathed in a Chinese-inspired sauce of ginger and soy. From this enticing marriage of culinary styles, our chefs create a new Asian classic.

 The flavors of this dish are set in a citrusy, yet lightly sweet frame, begging for the fresh character of **Sauvignon Blanc**. Our cellar choice, a Ferrari-Carano **Fumé Blanc** (Sauvignon Blanc) from Sonoma County, California, displays ripe fig flavors with light oak to pick up the sweeter aspects in the sauce. From France, a Château de Sancerre's Loire Valley **Sancerre** (Sauvignon Blanc) coaxes flavor out of the shiitakes with its mineral elements. The Cape Mentelle **Semillon/Sauvignon Blanc** from the Margaret River in Western Australia provides both roundness and a lovely grassy note that carries the vegetables well.

~ STIR-FRIED OPAKAPAKA ~
with Asian Vegetables and Soy-Ginger Sauce

Soy-Ginger Sauce

1 tablespoon vegetable oil

¼ cup light soy sauce

3 tablespoons rice vinegar

Juice of 1 fresh lemon

1 tablespoon chicken broth

1 tablespoon mirin (sweet sake) or
sweet sherry

1 teaspoon minced lemongrass

½ tablespoon minced garlic

½ tablespoon grated fresh ginger

2 tablespoons sugar

1 tablespoon cornstarch mixed with
1 tablespoon water

Asian Vegetables

2 ounces shiitake mushrooms, stemmed
and finely sliced

⅓ cup finely julienned red bell pepper

2 ounces snow peas

1 cup (about 12 ears) fresh baby corn

½ teaspoon Asian sesame oil

Salt & freshly ground white pepper

1 cup vegetable oil

4 baby eggplants, cut in half lengthwise

Opakapaka

½ teaspoon shichimi powder
(available in Japanese markets)
or regular chili powder

½ teaspoon salt

½ teaspoon ground white pepper

½ egg white, lightly beaten

2 teaspoons cornstarch

12 ounces opakapaka fillets, skin on,
cut into 12 slices

1 tablespoon vegetable oil

Garnish

Fresh cilantro sprigs

Serves 4

CHEF'S NOTES Opakapaka is a prestigious Hawaiian snapper with a light-pink medium-firm flesh. It may be substituted with red snapper or striped bass. If fresh baby corn is not available, jarred baby corn may be substituted.

PREPARATION To make the sauce: in a small saucepan, combine the oil, soy sauce, vinegar, lemon juice, broth, and mirin or sherry. Bring to a boil and add the lemongrass, garlic, ginger, and sugar. Reduce heat to very low and simmer for about 10 minutes. Stir the cornstarch mixture and add to the sauce. Cook the sauce for 5 more minutes, stirring occasionally. Taste and adjust the seasoning. Set aside.

To cook the vegetables: in a large saucepan of salted boiling water, blanch the mushrooms, bell pepper, snow peas, and baby corn for about 10 seconds. Drain well. In a small bowl, toss with sesame oil and salt and pepper to taste. Set aside and keep warm.

In a wok or a large nonstick sauté pan or skillet over high heat, heat the vegetable oil over high heat and fry the eggplant for about 30 seconds on each side, or until golden. Using a slotted metal spatula, transfer the eggplant slices to paper towels to drain. Set aside and keep warm.

To cook the opakapaka: in a small bowl, mix the shichimi or chili powder, salt, pepper, egg white, and cornstarch together. Dip the fish slices into this mixture to coat evenly. In a wok or a large nonstick skillet over high heat, heat the oil until almost smoking and fry the fish slices for about 30 seconds on each side, or until opaque throughout. Using a slotted spoon or wire-mesh skimmer, transfer to paper towels to drain.

TO SERVE Toss the fish slices with the sauce. Place some vegetables in the center of each plate. Arrange 3 slices of fish on each serving and top with 2 eggplant halves. Garnish with the cilantro and serve.

Asian fruit vendors arrange their exotic wares in bright pyramids: papaya, rambuttan, jack fruit, logan, dragon fruit. Such delicacies infuse our fruit kebabs with sweet tangs and subtle colors, varied by our chefs to match the specialties in each Asian port. The crisp, hot kebabs contrast the soft, cool pudding and orange fruit soup, for a surprising and delightful finish to the meal.

 A rainbow of sweet flavors requires exhilarating fruit in wine. The Kendall-Jackson **Late Harvest Chardonnay** from California displays apricot, honey, and lime notes against a caramel-oak backdrop, making it our cellar selection for the tantalizing tropical and citrus qualities of this dessert. Another fine choice is the Tim Adams **Semillon** from the Claire Valley of Australia, whose orange marmalade sweet/bitter aspect supports the tapioca pudding as it cleanses the palate.

~ TAPIOCA PUDDING ~
with Tempura Fruit Kabobs & Orange Fruit Soup

Tapioca Pudding

1 cup tapioca pearls

3 cups coconut milk

⅓ cup sugar

2 tablespoons unsalted butter

Pinch of salt

¼ teaspoon vanilla extract

Orange Fruit Soup

½ cup fresh orange juice

¼ cup Grand Marnier or other orange liqueur

Sugar to taste

1 tablespoon orange marmalade

4 fresh strawberries, hulled and finely diced

2 kiwifruits, peeled and finely diced

1 mango, peeled, cut from the pit, and finely diced

6 fresh mint leaves, finely julienned

Fruit Kabobs

Six ¾-inch fresh pineapple cubes

Six ¾-inch papaya cubes

Six ¾-inch mango cubes

Six ¾-inch honeydew melon cubes

6 small fresh strawberries, hulled

Sweet Tempura Batter (page 165)

4 cups vegetable oil for deep-frying

Cornstarch for dusting

Garnish

Ground cumin

Fresh mint sprigs

Makes 6 individual servings

CHEF'S NOTES To make this dish, you will need six 2½-inch-diameter plastic rings for molding the puddings, and six 6-inch bamboo skewers for the tempura, both available in kitchenware stores. To simplify this recipe, buy tempura batter mix and just add water.

PREPARATION To make the tapioca: preheat the oven to 400°F. In a small Dutch oven or medium flameproof casserole, combine the tapioca pearls and coconut milk and let sit at room temperature for at least 2 hours.

Add the sugar, butter, salt, and vanilla to the tapioca and bring the mixture to a boil, stirring constantly. Put the pan in the oven and bake, uncovered, until the liquid is completely evaporated, about 30 minutes.

Set aside to cool slightly, about 10 minutes. Refrigerate the pudding for about 30 minutes. Line a baking sheet with waxed paper and place six 2½-inch-diameter plastic rings on top. Fill the rings with the pudding. Smooth the tops with a spatula and refrigerate the puddings.

To make the soup: in a small saucepan, combine the orange juice, liqueur, sugar, and marmalade, and cook over medium heat until the marmalade is completely dissolved. Cook to reduce the liquid by one third. Strain through a fine-meshed sieve and let cool. Add all the fruits and the julienned mint. Set aside.

To make the kabobs: thread 1 pineapple cube, 1 papaya cube, 1 mango cube, 1 melon cube, and 1 strawberry on each of six 6-inch bamboo skewers.

Prepare the Sweet Tempura Batter (page 165). In a Dutch oven or deep fryer, heat the oil to 375°F. Dust the fruit kabobs with cornstarch, dip them into the tempura batter to coat evenly, and fry them for about 2 minutes, or until lightly browned. Using a slotted spoon or a wire-mesh skimmer, transfer to paper towels to drain.

TO SERVE Place a pudding in the center of each of 6 shallow soup bowls. Pour orange soup around each pudding. Place 1 fruit kabob on top. Sprinkle the rims of the bowls with cumin and garnish each with a mint sprig.

Mt. Fuji's majestic cone, rising through the clouds into the clear sunlit air, has inspired countless artists — including our Culinary Director. He evokes its snowy summit in a smooth, icy sorbet of herbal rosemary and subtly flavored sake. Its pure flavor and ethereal air received rave reviews from the culinary authorities of the renowned James Beard House.

The Latin name for rosemary is *Rosmarinus*, which means "dew of the sea." The name has never been more appropriate than in this distinctive dessert, where the fresh, aromatic flavors of the rosemary join the delicate sweetness of the sake sorbet. It should be served without wine, as a palate-cleanser between courses or as a refreshing finish to any Asian-inspired meal.

～ ROSEMARY-SAKE SORBET ～

Rosemary-Sake Sorbet

4 cups water

½ cup corn syrup

⅓ cup sugar

1¾ cups sake

10 fresh rosemary sprigs

Candied Rosemary

1 cup water

1 cup granulated sugar

Reserved rosemary sprigs from sorbet, above

10 tablespoons sake

Serves 10

CHEF'S NOTES This special sorbet may be served as a dessert or as a palate refresher between courses.

PREPARATION To make the sorbet: in a medium saucepan, combine the water, corn syrup, sugar, sake, and rosemary sprigs. Bring to a boil. Remove from heat, cover, and set aside for about 15 minutes to infuse the rosemary flavor.

Using a slotted spoon, transfer the rosemary sprigs to a plate. Pour the rosemary syrup into an ice cream maker and freeze according to the manufacturer's instructions.

To make the candied rosemary: in a small saucepan, combine the water and ½ cup of the sugar, and bring to a boil. Add the reserved rosemary sprigs and simmer very slowly over very low heat for about 4 hours, checking periodically to see if any water needs to be added to keep it from going dry. Using a slotted spoon, transfer the rosemary sprigs to a baking sheet lined with plastic wrap. Sprinkle to cover both sides with the remaining sugar.

TO SERVE Spoon the sorbet into serving dishes. Pour 1 tablespoon of the sake around each serving of sorbet and insert a candied rosemary sprig into the sorbet.

Celebration of Life The last golden rays

fade from the hillsides, as the sun sinks slowly into the harbor.
Townspeople stroll homeward in the pink twilight, chatting about
the day's events. Soon lights glow in every household, and the air
fills with laughter, greetings, the sounds of companionship around
a richly laid table. Here in the Mediterranean, a meal is an inte-
gral part of life's bounty: a celebration of friendship, conversation,
and ease. Because food is so important, Mediterraneans place
intense focus on quality ingredients, elevating simple things like
olive oil, vinegar, and paté to gourmet categories all their own.
The honest, natural flavors of the ingredients are exalted—
luscious *fruits de mer,* literally "fruits of the sea," truffles and
Porcini mushrooms from the forests, blood oranges and eggplants
ripening in mellow sunshine. Our chefs share this approach to
fine cuisine as a blend of science, craft, and creative intuition.
Even more important, they share the Mediterranean belief that
the pleasures of the table are an important part
of living well. As we cruise the Mediterranean, its
wondrous aromas fill our kitchens, its atmosphere
and gentle pace infuse the air.

"Dining in this region is more than just a meal...
it is an experience of relaxation and conversation
which brings every flavor and aroma to its peak."
—*Toni Neumeister*

Simple, pure flavors of sea and land, prepared with age-old skill. The scallops are seasoned with a pinch of sea salt, enhancing their mild sweetness. Vegetables fresh from the fertile soil are roasted to bring out their true character, and dressed with a dash of balsamic vinegar. Enjoyed with friends in mellow twilight, this country-style dish is an authentic Mediterranean experience.

 Satisfying and simple at the same time, the delicacy of scallops paired with the caramelized earthiness of roasted vegetables needs a wine with clean fruit to elevate the flavors. Flinty and crisp, the Groth **Sauvignon Blanc** from Napa Valley, California, is our choice against the herbal richness of the salad. A green apple-flavored **Vouvray** (Chenin Blanc) from France's Château Moncontour of the Loire Valley can brighten the sweet subtlety of the scallops. A fruitier choice that also picks up on the slight caramel-roasted notes is the Rombauer **Chardonnay** from the Carneros region of California.

∼ SEA SCALLOPS ∼
with Roasted Mediterranean Vegetable Salad

Roasted Vegetables

2 tablespoons extra-virgin olive oil

1 small yellow onion, finely chopped

3 shallots, finely sliced

4 garlic cloves, minced

3 small red bell peppers, seeded,
deribbed, and cut into ¼-inch dice

1 small green bell pepper, seeded,
deribbed, and cut into ¼-inch dice

1 zucchini, cut into ¼-inch dice

1 eggplant, cut into ¼-inch dice

8 fresh basil leaves, stemmed and
coarsely chopped

1 fresh thyme sprig

1 tablespoon tomato paste

1 pound fresh tomatoes, peeled, seeded,
and chopped (page 163), peels reserved

Pinch of cayenne pepper

Salt & freshly ground white pepper

Dressing

3 tablespoons Roasted Vegetables, above

2 tablespoons reserved pan juices from
Roasted Vegetables, above

1 tablespoon balsamic vinegar

Salt & freshly ground white pepper

Fried Garnish

2 cups vegetable oil for deep-frying

2 garlic cloves, finely sliced

4 large fresh basil leaves

4 sprigs curly parsley, stemmed

4 reserved tomato peels from Roasted
Vegetables, above

Salt & freshly ground white pepper

Scallops

12 large sea scallops

1 teaspoon sea salt

Garnish

Parmesan cheese shavings

1 tablespoon basil oil (page 158)

Serves 4

CHEF'S NOTES   In Europe, sea scallops are usually sold live and in their shells, in which case they are steamed. In North America, they are usually sold already shucked, and may be sautéed. Methods for both preparations are included in this recipe.

PREPARATION   To roast the vegetables: preheat the oven to 300°F. In a large ovenproof nonstick sauté pan or skillet over low heat, heat the oil and sauté the onion, shallots, and garlic until translucent, about 3 minutes. Increase heat to medium and add the bell peppers, zucchini, and eggplant. Sauté for about 3 minutes, or until the vegetables are softened. Add the herbs and cook for about 2 minutes. Add the tomato paste, tomatoes, cayenne, and salt and pepper to taste and cook, stirring constantly, for about 1 minute.

Remove the pan from heat and cover with aluminum foil. Place the pan in the oven and roast for about 30 minutes, or until the vegetables are soft to the touch. Remove from the oven, uncover, and let cool slightly. Drain the vegetables, reserving the pan juices. Set aside.

To make the dressing: combine all the ingredients in a blender, using the salt and pepper to taste, and blend until smooth.

To fry the garnish: heat the oil to 350°F in a Dutch oven or large skillet. Separately fry the garlic, basil, parsley, and tomato peels for about 20 seconds each, or until crisp. Using a slotted spoon or a wire-mesh skimmer, transfer each ingredient to paper towels to drain. In a medium bowl, mix all the fried garnishes together. Season with salt and pepper to taste.

To cook the scallops: if the scallops are in the shell, wash them well and pat dry with paper towels. Steam them over boiling water in a covered pan for about 2 minutes, or until the shells are wide open and the scallops are opaque throughout. If the scallops are shucked, pat them dry with a paper towel. In a large nonstick sauté pan or skillet over high heat, sear the scallops for about 1 minute on each side, or until lightly browned. Sprinkle with sea salt and set aside.

TO SERVE   Spoon 2 tablespoons of the roasted vegetables into the center of each plate or use a cylindrical mold to form a tower. Spoon the dressing around the base of the vegetable salad and decorate the top with the fried garnish and Parmesan shavings. Place 3 scallops on each plate and sprinkle a few drops of basil oil around them.

The chefs of ancient Rome found that snails fed on vine leaves were the most succulent of all. Today, Burgundy's manicured vineyards produce not only fabled wines, but the world's best escargots as well. We bathe these tender little mollusks in another French classic, the sinfully smooth herbal elixir of Provençal Butter. A star of our French Night celebrations.

Wonderfully buttery and garlicky, these little gems require a clean dry wine to bathe the palate in cleansing acidity, preparing it for the next bite. Our classic pairing is from the south of France: the Domaine l'Hortus, Côte de Provence **Rosé** (Grenache/Syrah/Mourvedre) from Pic St-Loup, with its peppery, crisp rose hip flavors. The Domaine Laroche "les Fourchaumes" **Chablis Premier Cru** (Chardonnay) from Burgundy, France, has a similar effect, with mirroring herbal notes. Napa Valley's Niebaum-Coppola "Edizione Pennino" **Zinfandel** shows the requisite acidity to cut through the butter while enhancing the spice quality of the dish.

~ ESCARGOTS ~
with Provençal Butter

1½ cups (3 sticks) unsalted butter at room temperature

4 garlic cloves, minced

3 small shallots, minced

½ cup minced fresh curly parsley

½ teaspoon Cognac or Brandy

½ teaspoon minced fresh rosemary

½ teaspoon minced fresh thyme

½ teaspoon minced fresh oregano

Salt & freshly ground white pepper

1 teaspoon demi-glace (optional, page 161)

Escargots

1 tablespoon Provençal Butter, above

½ small shallot, minced

½ garlic clove, minced

24 canned French escargots (snails), preferably from Burgundy, drained

Salt & freshly ground white pepper

1 tablespoon Cognac or Brandy

Serves 4

CHEF'S NOTES The Provençal butter tastes even better when prepared 1 day ahead.

PREPARATION To make the butter: in a small bowl, combine all the ingredients and mix until well blended, using the salt and pepper to taste. Use now, or cover and refrigerate, preferably overnight.

To make the escargots: preheat the oven to 400°F. In a medium sauté pan or skillet, melt the butter over medium heat and sauté the shallots and garlic until translucent, about 2 minutes. Add the escargots and sauté for about 1 minute. Season with salt and pepper to taste, and cook for 2 minutes. Add the Cognac or Brandy, heat for a moment, avert your face, and light with a long-handled match. Shake the pan until the flames subside.

TO SERVE Place the escargots in escargot dishes. Spread a spoonful of the Provençal butter over each escargot. Place the dishes in the oven and bake for 8 to 10 minutes, or until the butter is bubbling.

Italians shape pasta in countless ways, and fill it with every imaginable delicacy, savory and sweet. Yet in this universe of delicious choices, a few classics stand out, like these ravioli filled with tender ricotta cheese and spinach. Our chefs add a unique sauce of Sicilian blood oranges, whose ruby-red color and exciting berry flavor capture the passion of Italy in one gorgeous dish.

The flavors of this dish call for a wine with great fruit combined with a firm structure. The perfect choice is a Renato Ratti **Dolcetto d'Alba** from Piedmont in northern Italy. It shows great purity of cherry-like, spicy fruit, standing up to the dish's exuberance. Also from Tuscany, Italy, the Case Basse, **Brunello di Montalcino Riserva** (Sangiovese) displays riper flavors to balance the richness of the ricotta. A Cuvaison "Carneros Reserve" **Chardonnay** from the Napa Valley, with supple, vanilla flavors, lends a roundness to the tangy notes of this dish.

~ RAVIOLI OF SPINACH & RICOTTA ~
with Blood Orange-Tomato Sauce

Ravioli

1 tablespoon extra-virgin olive oil

1 shallot, minced

1 small garlic clove, minced

*8 cups packed spinach leaves
(about 1 bunch)*

Pinch of ground nutmeg

Salt & freshly ground white pepper

*2 tablespoons pine nuts, toasted and
coarsely chopped (page 165)*

*2 large fresh basil leaves, finely
julienned*

¼ cup ricotta cheese

*Forty-eight 4-inch-square wonton
wrappers*

Blood Orange-Tomato Sauce

½ tablespoon olive oil

1 shallot, minced

1 small garlic clove, minced

2 fresh basil leaves, coarsely chopped

*½ cup fresh blood orange or regular
orange juice*

2 cups tomato juice

Salt & freshly ground white pepper

2 tablespoons unsalted butter

½ tablespoon extra-virgin olive oil

½ tablespoon butter

Garnish

Fresh basil leaves, finely julienned

Fresh flat-leaf (Italian) parsley sprigs

Serves 4

CHEF'S NOTES Blood oranges, usually available in the winter months, give the sauce in this recipe a special berry-like flavor, but regular oranges may be substituted. The sauce is also excellent with sautéed sea scallops and white-fleshed fish such as halibut. At Crystal Cruises, we make our pasta from scratch, but wonton sheets are an excellent substitute.

PREPARATION To make the ravioli: in a medium saucepan over medium heat, heat the oil and sauté the shallot and garlic for about 2 minutes, or until translucent. Add the spinach, nutmeg, and salt and pepper to taste and sauté for 2 to 3 minutes. Set aside and let cool.

Chop the spinach finely by hand (not in a food processor). Place in a small bowl and add the remaining filling ingredients.

Place 24 wonton sheets on a semolina flour-dusted work surface. Put 1 tablespoon filling in the center of each sheet. With a pastry brush dipped in water, brush around the filling. Place each of the remaining sheets over a sheet with filling. Using a 3½-inch round pasta cutter, seal each ravioli by cutting out a round ravioli. Dust a large plate or tray with semolina flour and carefully place the ravioli on it, making sure they do not touch.

To make the sauce: in a heavy, medium saucepan over medium heat, heat the oil and sauté the shallot, garlic, and basil for about 3 minutes, or until the shallot and garlic are translucent. Add the orange juice, bring to a boil, and cook to reduce by half. Add the tomato juice and cook to reduce by half. Season with salt and pepper to taste. Strain through a fine-meshed sieve into a bowl, then return to the saucepan and bring to a boil. Remove from heat and whisk in the butter. Taste and adjust the seasoning, and keep warm.

Add the olive oil to a large pot of salted boiling water. Reduce heat to a gentle boil and add the ravioli. Cook for about 3 minutes, or until al dente. Drain the ravioli, put them in a pasta bowl, and add the butter, turning them gently to coat with the butter. Add the sauce and gently turn the ravioli to coat them.

TO SERVE Divide the ravioli among warm pasta bowls. Garnish with the basil and parsley. Serve immediately.

Mushrooms are the subtle treasures of the forest, emerging from the moist earth in a dazzling variety of flavors and textures: nutty, earthy tastes and delicate earth tones, ridged, ruffled, pitted, and smooth. We use a rich cream sauce to accentuate the full, distinct flavors of the porcini, portobellos, and morels, then serve in a fragrant bread cup still warm from the oven. Delizioso!

Nutty, mild, and rich, this soup requires a wine that is reflective of its character. Our cellar choice, the Terruzzi e Puthod **Vernaccia** from San Gimignano in Tuscany, Italy, mirrors the mild mushroom flavors with elegant fruit and a hint of oak. The Emilio Lustau **Amontillado Sherry** from the Jerez region of Spain has a nutty flavor that underscores its dry, lean character and picks up on the soup's rounder aspects. And finally, the Byron **Pinot Noir** from Santa Barbara County, California, has the red-fruited, earth-laden succulence that mushrooms seem to have been created for.

Soup

1 ounce dried morels, or 2 ounces fresh morels

3 tablespoons extra-virgin olive oil

½ cup portobello mushroom, finely sliced

2 ounces white mushrooms

3 ounces fresh porcini mushrooms, finely sliced

3 shallots, minced

2 garlic cloves, minced

Salt & freshly ground white pepper

½ cup dry white wine

4 cups chicken stock (page 159)

½ cup heavy cream

2 tablespoons minced fresh flat-leaf (Italian) parsley

Leaves from 1 fresh thyme sprig, minced

Leaves from 1 fresh oregano sprig, minced

2 large fresh basil leaves, chopped

Four 6-inch round bread loaves

Garnish

Fresh rosemary sprigs

Serves 4

CHEF'S NOTES At Crystal Cruises we serve this soup in oregano bread cups. Any plain or flavored bread loaf may be substituted, but this soup is also delicious simply served in shallow soup bowls.

PREPARATION If using dried morels, wash the caps and soak them in warm water to cover for 10 minutes. Remove the stems and discard them. Cut small morels in half and large ones into 3 or 4 pieces.

In a medium saucepan over medium heat, heat the olive oil and sauté all the mushrooms for about 3 minutes. Add the shallots and garlic and sauté for 2 minutes. Season with salt and pepper to taste, add the wine, and cook to reduce the liquid by half. Add the stock and bring to a boil. Add the cream and bring to a boil. Reduce heat, cover, and simmer the soup for about 25 minutes. In a blender or food processor, purée half the soup until very smooth. Return the purée to the pan. Stir in the parsley, thyme, oregano, and basil and cook for about 2 minutes. Taste and adjust the seasoning. Keep warm.

TO SERVE Preheat the oven to 200°F. Cut off the top of each bread loaf. With a large spoon, remove the soft inner part of the bread. Place the loaves on a baking pan and warm in the oven for about 5 minutes. Remove the warm bread loaves from the oven and pour the hot soup into the bread cups. Garnish with the rosemary sprigs and serve.

*Italy's soups evoke the moods and personality of that
irresistible country: honest and down-to-earth, made
according to family recipes, still in tune with the seasons
of Nature and the rhythms of the farm. In our silky-
textured rendition of Trieste's famed zuppa di lenticchie,
lentils lend a smoky meatiness that exalts the dense pork
flavors of the pancetta.*

A wine with brisk fruit, and
minimal oak and tannin
influence highlights the rustic
qualities of this soup. Our
choice for this dish is a vibrant
Zinfandel from Ridge
Vineyards in Dry Creek Valley, Sonoma
County, California, with rich blackberry
fruit and spice. The Arnaldo Caprai
"25 Anni" **Sagrantino di Montefalco**
in the Umbria region of Italy shows more
power with similar intense fruit character.
An interesting companion to lentils is
the Dopff & Irion **Gewürztraminer**
"Les Sorcières" from Alsace, France.
Rich, spicy, and aromatic, it accents the
smoky aspects of the soup beautifully.

～ COUNTRY-STYLE LENTIL SOUP ～
with Pancetta

½ tablespoon unsalted butter

¼ cup diced pancetta

1 onion, finely chopped

4 shallots, minced

2 garlic cloves, minced

1 cup finely diced carrot

⅓ celery stalk, diced

½ cup minced fresh flat-leaf (Italian) parsley

1 cup French lentils, picked over, rinsed, and soaked in cold water for 2 hours

1 tablespoon tomato paste

5 cups chicken stock (page 159)

2 large tomatoes, seeded and diced (page 163)

Bouquet garni (page 158)

1 teaspoon Dijon mustard

1 tablespoon balsamic vinegar

Salt & freshly ground white pepper

Serves 4

CHEF'S NOTES To serve as a vegetarian soup, omit the pancetta and replace the chicken stock with vegetable stock (page 166).

PREPARATION In a soup pot, melt the butter over medium heat and sauté the pancetta for 1 minute. Add the onion, shallots, and garlic, and sauté until the onion is translucent, 2 to 3 minutes. Add the carrot and celery and sauté for 1 minute. Add half the parsley and cook for about 1 minute. Stir in the lentils and tomato paste and cook for 2 more minutes. Add the stock, tomatoes, and bouquet garni. Bring to a boil, reduce heat, and simmer, uncovered, for about 25 minutes, or until the lentils are tender. Add the mustard, vinegar, salt and pepper to taste, and the remaining parsley.

TO SERVE Serve in shallow soup bowls.

The heart and soul of this soup is its fresh Mediterranean flavors: basil, bell peppers, plump tomatoes, a head of garlic, and fragrant spices, along with Japanese eggplant from our wealth of international ingredients. We roast this bounty to create its smoky subtlety, season with extra-virgin olive oil and aged Parmesan, then purée to a fine russet color and creamy consistency.

Vibrancy and delicate toastiness in equal doses call for a wine that has immense fruit, but not a wine that is soft or overtly oaky. Our cellar selection is the Duca di Salaparuta **Corvo Rosso** (Nevello Mascalese/ Perricone/Nero d'Avola) from Sicily, Italy, that offers fruity cherry and strawberry character to balance the high tones of the soup. The Acacia **Pinot Noir** from the Carneros region of Napa Valley, California, has equally fine red-fruited features and highlights the basil notes with a slight herbal pitch. A wonderful contrast to the earthy richness on the palate is a brisk, citrusy Santa Margherita **Pinot Grigio** from Alto Adige, Italy.

1 unpeeled head garlic

1 large Japanese eggplant

2 unpeeled yellow onions

1 red bell pepper

2 tomatoes

1 tablespoon extra-virgin olive oil

10 fresh basil leaves

½ tablespoon minced fresh oregano

Salt & freshly ground white pepper

4 cups chicken stock (page 159)

¼ cup grated Parmesan cheese

1 tablespoon unsalted butter

Serves 4

CHEF'S NOTES The flavor of this soup is enhanced by making the soup 1 day ahead. For a vegetarian soup, replace the chicken stock with vegetable stock. The soup can also be served cold.

PREPARATION Preheat the oven to 375°F. Cut the garlic head in half crosswise. Pierce the eggplant in several places with a fork. Put the garlic, eggplant, onions, and bell pepper on a baking sheet and roast in the oven until tender, about 20 minutes. Add the tomatoes and continue to roast for another 20 minutes. Remove the vegetables from the oven and let cool to the touch. Peel, halve, and seed the tomato and bell pepper. Cut the eggplant in half, spoon out the pulp, and discard the skin. Peel the onions and set aside. Push the garlic pulp out of the cloves by pressing each clove between your fingers. Cut all the vegetables into medium pieces.

In a large saucepan over medium heat, heat the olive oil. Add the roasted vegetables, basil, and oregano. Season with salt and pepper to taste. Cook for about 5 minutes. Add 3 cups of the stock, bring to a boil, reduce heat, and simmer the soup for about 15 minutes. In a blender or food processor, in batches if necessary, purée the soup.

Return the purée to the saucepan and add the remaining 1 cup stock. Bring to a boil, reduce heat, and simmer for about 5 minutes. Stir in the Parmesan and butter. Taste and adjust the seasoning.

TO SERVE Serve in shallow soup bowls.

For centuries, meat dishes in the noble kitchens of France were seasoned with a hint of bitter Seville oranges from neighboring Spain. Thus one of the legends of French grande cuisine was born: Canard à l'Orange, an ornament to the most elegant tables in the world. The secret of this famed recipe is a perfect balance between the bitter, tart orange, and the sweetness of duck and its sauce.

Duck is best paired with an intense red wine with soft tannins. The cherry-infused elegance of the Louis Jadot "Clos de Bèzes" **Chambertin** (Pinot Noir), from Burgundy, France, is our cellar selection. An equally delicious **Pinot Noir** from California's Russian River is the Gary Farrell from Allen Vineyard, with a core of red fruit and a slight orange-peel note. From Spain, the **Rioja Reserva** (Tempranillo) from Marqués de Griñón presents a vanillin-flavored, berry counterpart to the tangy flavors surrounding the duck.

~ ROASTED DUCK ~
with Orange Sauce & Amandine Pears

Duck

2 ducks, about 4 pounds each

Orange Sauce

1½ cups fresh orange juice

1 tablespoon Grand Marnier or other orange liqueur

2 tablespoons sugar

⅓ cup sherry vinegar

Julienned zest of ½ orange

3 cups duck stock (page 161)

Salt & freshly ground black pepper

2 tablespoons unsalted butter

Amandine Pears

1 large russet potato, peeled, scrubbed, and cut into large cubes

1 egg yolk

Salt & freshly ground white pepper

2 tablespoons flour, plus more for dusting

2 tablespoons sliced almonds

1 egg white, lightly beaten

1 cup blanched almonds, chopped

3 cups vegetable oil for deep-frying

Orange Garnish (page 163)

Salt & freshly ground black pepper

2 teaspoons extra-virgin olive oil

1½ cups duck stock (page 161)

Serves 4

CHEF'S NOTES Seville oranges provide a tartness which balances the sweetness of the other ingredients in this recipe. Navel oranges with a little lime juice may be substituted.

PREPARATION Cut the breasts and legs from each duck. Cut the legs into 2 parts at the joint. Remove all visible fat. Use the duck carcasses and fat to make the duck stock (page 161).

To make the sauce: in a small, heavy saucepan, combine the orange juice, liqueur, and sugar. Bring to a boil over medium heat and cook until caramelized. Remove the pan from heat and stir in the vinegar and the zest. Return to medium heat, bring to a boil, and cook until reduced by two thirds. Add the stock and cook to reduce by half. Strain through a fine-meshed sieve into a saucepan. Add the salt and pepper to taste. Return to a boil, remove from heat, and whisk in the butter. Set aside and keep warm.

To make the Almondine Pears: cook the potato in salted boiling water until tender, about 20 minutes. Drain the potato well and put it in a small bowl. Mash the potato with a whisk. Whisk in the egg yolk and salt and pepper to taste. Blend in the 2 tablespoons flour until thoroughly blended. Add the almonds and mix well. Divide the dough into 8 parts and form each into a pear shape. Dust each "pear" with flour, dip in the beaten egg white, and coat with the chopped almonds.

In a Dutch oven or deep fryer, heat the oil to 375°F. Using a slotted spoon, add the "pears" to the oil and deep-fry until golden brown, about 2 minutes. Using the slotted spoon, transfer to paper towels to drain. Set aside and keep warm.

Prepare the Orange Garnish (page 163).

To cook the duck: preheat the oven to 400°F. Season the duck meat with salt and pepper to taste. In a large, heavy ovenproof sauté pan or skillet over medium heat, heat the olive oil and sear the breasts (skin-side down), legs, and thighs until well browned. Remove the breasts; set aside and keep warm. Place the pan in the oven and roast the legs and thighs for about 15 minutes. Return the breasts and continue roasting for 5 minutes. Add 1 cup of the stock and roast for about 10 more minutes, basting occasionally. Add the remaining ½ cup stock and roast 10 minutes longer, basting occasionally. Remove from the oven. Set aside and keep warm.

Add half the julienned orange zest garnish to the orange sauce. Reheat the sauce. Taste and adjust the seasoning.

TO SERVE Slice the duck breasts into 3 slices. Place a leg and thigh in the center of each plate. Cut the breasts into slices and place alongside the legs. Drizzle with the orange sauce. Place two Amandine Pears around the duck and garnish with the orange segments and the remaining orange zest.

In the warm glow of evening, fishermen sit mending their nets, having drawn a rich catch from the bright blue waves. One of their best prizes is the Daurade Royale, found only in these waters. Here this elegant, fine-fleshed fish, with its gorgeously textured skin, nestles amid a luscious Provençal preparation of basil, browned butter, olives, and roasted tomatoes: a Mediterranean classic.

A wine with zesty elements balanced by a graceful weight provides the perfect complement to the flavors of this dish. Our cellar selection is a Pinot Noir, the François Charles "Clos de la Cave" **Volnay** from Burgundy, France. Its impeccable balance lends focus to the roasted tomato flavors without overwhelming the fish. The Château du Nozet "de Ladoucette" **Pouilly-Fumé** (Sauvignon Blanc) from France's Loire Valley offers tart citrus and herbal notes to cleanse the palate as well as mirror the flavors of the Daurade. A New World alternative offering similar characteristics is the Carmenet **Sauvignon Blanc** from Sonoma Valley, California.

~ PAN-ROASTED DAURADE ROYALE ~
with Slow-Roasted Tomatoes & Brown Butter-Basil Sauce

Slow-Roasted Tomatoes (page 164)

Brown Butter-Basil Sauce

4 tablespoons unsalted butter

2 cups chicken stock (page 159)

3 tablespoons brown veal stock (page 158)

Reserved cooking juices from Slow-Roasted Tomatoes, above

4 kalamata olives, pitted, cut into strips, and roasted for about 4 minutes in a preheated 250°F oven

4 large fresh basil leaves, finely julienned

Freshly ground white pepper to taste

Daurade

4 Daurade Royale fillets, skin on, about 6 ounces each

Salt & freshly ground white pepper

2 tablespoons extra-virgin olive oil

2 tablespoons chopped flat-leaf (Italian) parsley

Serves 4

CHEF'S NOTES Daurade Royale is a Mediterranean sea bream, which has a firm white flesh. Red snapper or sea bass may be substituted.

PREPARATION Prepare the Slow-Roasted Tomatoes (page 164), reserving the juices for the sauce. Set aside and keep warm.

To make the sauce: in a small saucepan, melt 2 tablespoons of the butter over medium heat and cook until the butter is nut brown, about 2 minutes. Remove from heat, add the remaining 2 tablespoons butter, and let it melt.

In a small saucepan, bring the chicken stock to a boil and cook to reduce by two thirds. Add the veal stock and cook to reduce the liquid by half again. Pour the liquid into a blender or food processor. With the machine running, pour in the reserved tomato cooking juices, then the browned butter. Return the sauce to the saucepan. Stir in the olives, basil, and pepper to taste. Set aside and keep warm.

To cook the daurade: preheat the oven to 375°F. Lightly score the skin side of each fillet in a grid pattern. Sprinkle the fish with salt and pepper to taste, 1 tablespoon of the olive oil, and the parsley. In a large ovenproof nonstick sauté pan or skillet over medium-high heat, heat the remaining 1 tablespoon oil and sear the fillets, skin-side down, for 1 minute. Turn and sear on the second side for 1 minute, or until lightly browned. Place the pan in the oven and bake for 3 to 4 minutes, or until opaque throughout.

TO SERVE Place the tomatoes in the center of each plate. Top with a fillet. Pour the warm sauce around the fish.

Emilia-Romagna is Italy's culinary heartland, and its slow-cooked pasta specialties inspired this epic dish. Layers of tender lasagne enfold the mellow meatiness of the Bolognese sauce, and a heavenly medley of woody porcini and other wild mushrooms. This dish takes a whole day to prepare, but its intoxicating aromas and the delighted sighs of our guests make it all worthwhile.

Meaty foods call for supple wines that deliver the structure necessary to unlock the flavors of the dish. The complex, slightly earthy Fontodi **Chianti Classico Riserva** (Sangiovese blend) from Tuscany, Italy, does just that, delivering structure while drawing out the mushroom flavors. Or, try a similarly blended Moroder "Dorico" **Rosso Conero** (Montepulciano/ Sangiovese) from Marches, Italy, a spicier alternative offering balance with ripe texture. A smoky white such as the Beringer "Private Reserve" **Chardonnay** from the Napa Valley of California coaxes sweetness from the sauce.

~ PREGO LASAGNE ~
with Bolognese & Mushroom Sauces

Bolognese Sauce

2 pounds ground beef chuck

¼ cup extra-virgin olive oil

1 large onion, diced

4 garlic cloves, coarsely chopped

1 large carrot, peeled and finely diced

2 celery stalks, finely diced

Salt & freshly ground white pepper

8 ounces fresh tomatoes, peeled, seeded, and coarsely chopped (page 163)

4 cups canned or packaged chopped tomatoes (preferably Italian or organic), including juice

2 tablespoons tomato paste

1 cup dry red wine

¼ cup packed fresh basil leaves, coarsely chopped

1 tablespoon minced fresh thyme

2 tablespoons minced fresh oregano

¼ cup minced fresh flat-leaf parsley

Mushroom Sauce

3 tablespoons extra-virgin olive oil

3 oyster mushrooms, coarsely sliced

3 portobello mushrooms, coarsely sliced

6 ounces porcini mushrooms, coarsely sliced

4 ounces white mushrooms, coarsely sliced

Salt & freshly ground white pepper

1 cup heavy cream

Lasagne

1 pound pre-cooked lasagne noodles

1 cup (4 ounces) grated Parmesan cheese

2 cups (8 ounces) shredded mozzarella

Tomato-Basil Sauce (page 165)

Alfredo Sauce (page 158)

Garnish

Fresh flat-leaf (Italian) parsley sprigs

Fresh basil sprigs

Serves 8

CHEF'S NOTES We recommend assembly 1 day before baking to allow the pasta to soften.

PREPARATION To make the Bolognese Sauce: preheat oven to 375°F. Spread the ground meat out on a sided baking sheet and put in the oven to cook for about 15 minutes, stirring frequently. Remove from the oven and set aside, leaving the oven on. Drain off the fat.

In a medium stockpot over medium heat, heat the oil and sauté the onion and garlic until translucent, about 3 minutes. Add the carrot and the celery and sauté for about 5 minutes. Season with salt and pepper to taste. Add the ground meat, fresh tomatoes, canned or packaged tomatoes and juice, and the tomato paste and stir well. Stir in the wine, basil, thyme, oregano, and parsley. Cover with aluminum foil, place in the oven, and bake for about 45 minutes. Let cool slightly. Taste and adjust the seasoning.

To make the Mushroom Sauce: in a large sauté pan or skillet over high heat, heat the oil and sauté the mushrooms for about 4 minutes, or until lightly browned. Season with salt and pepper to taste. Add the cream and cook to reduce by half. Stir the mushroom sauce into the bolognese sauce until thoroughly mixed.

ASSEMBLY Spread ¼ inch of the sauce mixture in the bottom of a 9-by-12-inch baking dish. Layer 3 lasagne noodles lengthwise over the mixture, overlapping the noodles slightly. Spread the noodles with one fourth of the remaining sauce. Sprinkle with one third of the Parmesan. Repeat the layering two times. Top with 3 lasagne noodles and spread them with the remaining sauce. Cover with plastic wrap and refrigerate for at least 2 hours, or preferably overnight.

Meanwhile, prepare the Tomato-Basil Sauce (page 165) and Alfredo Sauce (page 158).

Remove the dish from the refrigerator 30 minutes before baking. Preheat the oven to 350°F. Sprinkle the lasagne with the mozzarella cheese. Cover with aluminum foil and bake for 30 minutes. Remove the foil and bake for 15 minutes, or until the cheese is melted and the lasagne is bubbling around the edges. Remove from the oven and let rest for 15 minutes before cutting.

TO SERVE Cut the lasagne into serving portions and serve in warm pasta bowls. Spoon the Tomato-Basil and Alfredo sauces around the lasagne and garnish with the herb sprigs.

Step into any one of the cozy little trattorie along the Grand Canal, and you immediately encounter this local favorite, which the Venetians love even more than pasta. The rich, creamy risotto is infused with dark, dramatic squid ink, and covered in mussels, squid, and clams—the authentic bounty of the Adriatic, whose waters are so much a part of life in Venice.

 The briny flavors of the sea combined with risotto's familiar creaminess provide a wonderful match for fruit-forward wines. Our cellar selection, the Castello Banfi "Centine" **Rosso di Montalcino** (Sangiovese blend) from Tuscany, Italy, combines concentrated red-cherry fruit with a medium body to balance the strong elements of the dish. The Duckhorn **Sauvignon Blanc** from Napa Valley, California, and the Umani Ronchi "Casal di Serra" **Verdicchio**, from Castelli di Jesi Classico in the Marches region of Italy, both offer cleansing, citrusy qualities that stand up to the creaminess of the risotto while offering a refreshing backdrop to the seafood.

~ BLACK INK RISOTTO ~
with Frutti di Mare

Marinated Seafood

6 fresh basil leaves, finely chopped

1 tablespoon minced fresh flat-leaf
(Italian) parsley

1 garlic clove, minced

Pinch of red pepper flakes

2 ½ tablespoons extra-virgin olive oil

Salt & freshly ground white pepper

8 sea scallops

8 large shrimp, shelled and deveined,
with tails

4 ounces squid, cleaned and cut
into strips

½ cup dry white wine

2 ounces black mussels, scrubbed and
debearded

2 ounces clams, scrubbed

Black Ink Risotto

5 cups chicken stock (page 159)

1 tablespoon squid ink

½ tablespoon extra-virgin olive oil

1 onion, finely chopped

2 cups Arborio rice

½ dry white wine

2 tablespoons unsalted butter

Salt & freshly ground white pepper

Garnish

1 tablespoon minced fresh flat-leaf
(Italian) parsley

Fresh flat-leaf (Italian) parsley sprigs

Serves 4

CHEF'S NOTES Squid ink is available in Italian food stores and some specialty foods markets.

PREPARATION To marinate the seafood: in a glass baking dish, combine all the ingredients for the marinade, using the salt and pepper to taste. Add the scallops, shrimp, and squid to the marinade, stir to coat, and let sit at room temperature for about 1 hour.

In a small saucepan, bring the wine to a boil. Add the mussels and clams, cover, and cook for about 3 minutes, or until the shellfish open. Discard any that do not open. Reserve the broth for cooking the risotto. Set shellfish aside and keep warm.

To make the risotto: in a small saucepan, combine the chicken stock, squid ink, and reserved shellfish broth from above, and bring to a boil. Set aside and keep warm. In a heavy, medium saucepan over low heat, heat the olive oil and sauté the onion until translucent, about 2 minutes. Add the rice and stir well for about 1 minute. Add the wine, bring to a boil, and cook to reduce by half.

Reduce the heat to low. Add 1 cup of the stock mixture and cook, stirring constantly, until the liquid is absorbed. Repeat the process 2 more times and cook until the rice is al dente, a total cooking time of about 30 to 35 minutes. If more liquid is needed to finish cooking the rice, add stock as needed. Stir in the butter until melted.

Pour the scallops, shrimp, squid, and their marinade into a large sauté pan or skillet. Bring the marinade to a boil over medium heat and cook until the scallops and squid are opaque and the shrimp are pink, about 2 minutes. Add the mussels and clams and cook a few seconds to reheat. Season with salt and pepper to taste.

TO SERVE Place the risotto in the center of each plate. Arrange the seafood on top and around the risotto. Drizzle with the remaining pan liquid from the seafood. Garnish with the minced parsley and parsley sprigs.

For Charles Dale, every voyage brings new cooking inspiration. He gathers ideas and insights as he travels the world, then returns home to his acclaimed Renaissance restaurant in Aspen, Colorado, to synthesize what he's learned in his own creative style. He began his career in France, and has evolved a distinctive New World French style. This dish, an authoritative tuna and red wine creation, is a favorite when Chef Dale conducts his Guest Chef Dinners on board.

Tuna is a dense meaty fish that is wonderfully embellished by a red wine with bright, fruit-forward character. This preparation adds a depth that also fits wines of intensity and weight. We chose a Dubreuil-Fontaine **Pernand-Vergelesses Rouge** (Pinot Noir) from Burgundy, France, with vibrant, red-cherry flavors and elegant texture to match the fish. The smoky spice of the Penfolds "Grange" **Shiraz** (Syrah) from South Australia or the elegant plum-berry character of the St. Francis **Merlot** from Sonoma County, California. Both are powerful wines that highlight the richness and depth of the shallots and Bordelaise Sauce.

SEARED TUNA WITH MASHED POTATOES, CARAMELIZED SHALLOTS & SAUCE BORDELAISE

A recipe from Charles Dale

Marinated Tuna

1 small bunch fresh thyme

1 small bunch fresh rosemary

2 garlic cloves, minced

¼ teaspoon freshly ground white pepper

⅓ cup extra-virgin olive oil

6 ahi tuna loins, preferably center cut,
5 ounces each

Caramelized Shallots

12 large shallots

¼ cup sugar

3 tablespoons butter

¼ teaspoon salt

½ cup water

Sauce Bordelaise

1 tablespoon extra-virgin olive oil

6 chicken wings

2 shallots, minced

2 cups dry red wine

3 cups chicken stock (page 159)

1 fresh thyme sprig

Mashed Potatoes

3 large russet potatoes

Salt

½ cup heavy cream

4 tablespoons unsalted butter

¼ cup milk

Salt

2 tablespoons extra-virgin olive oil

Garnish

Fresh thyme sprigs

Serves 6

CHEF'S NOTES Sometimes after being at the stove on a busy night, I feel like eating something homey and comforting. Aspen winters can be bone-chilling, and mashed potatoes always warm the soul. The herbs and shallots give this dish the characteristics of a great steak. Use high-quality, fresh tuna and cook it rare to medium-rare.

PREPARATION In a glass baking dish just big enough to hold the tuna, combine the herbs, garlic, pepper, and oil. Add the tuna, turn to coat, cover, and refrigerate for 1 hour, turning once or twice.

To caramelize the shallots: in a medium sauté pan or skillet, combine all the shallot ingredients. Cook over high heat until the water evaporates and the sugar begins to caramelize, tossing the shallots frequently so they are uniformly coated. Set aside and keep warm.

To make the sauce: in a large, heavy saucepan over medium heat, heat the olive oil and sauté the chicken wings until browned on both sides. Add the minced shallots and sauté for 1 minute. Add the wine and cook until almost completely evaporated, about 10 minutes. Immediately add the stock and thyme. Cook to reduce to 1 cup of liquid; this may take up to 30 minutes. Strain the sauce through a fine-meshed sieve. Spoon off as much fat as possible. Add the sauce to the caramelized shallots. Set aside and keep warm.

To make the potatoes: in a large pot of salted boiling water, cook the potatoes until tender, about 20 minutes; the blade of a paring knife should pass easily through the center of each potato. Drain.

Holding the hot potatoes in a towel, peel off the skins. Meanwhile, bring the cream, butter, and milk to a boil, seasoning with salt to taste; set aside and keep warm. Cut the potatoes into chunks and pass them through a potato ricer into a warm bowl. Or, mash them in the pot they were cooked in, using a potato masher. Add the hot cream mixture and stir until blended. Set aside and keep warm.

Remove the tuna from the marinade and sprinkle it with salt to taste. In a large sauté pan or skillet over high heat, heat the oil and sear the tuna for about 1 minute on each side.

TO SERVE Spoon the mashed potatoes in the center of each plate. Cut each loin into 3 slices and arrange the slices around the potatoes. Spoon the shallots and sauce around the tuna and garnish with the thyme sprigs.

In bustling alleyways of a North African bazaar, our chefs select the ingredients for this exciting Moroccan stew: amber cumin, red cayenne, and ochre turmeric, slender saffron threads, bowls of olives, lemons steeped in their own juice. They blend these vibrant flavors and textures in a tagine, a porcelain dish with a long tradition in this fascinating Mediterranean realm.

Racy flavors such as these are beautifully framed by a wine that is bold and complex. We chose California's Cline Cellars Sonoma/Carneros **Roussanne** for its ability to match the dish with stony, floral aromas, and delicate oak notes. Another fine option is the Caves São João **Bairrada Frei João Reserva** (Baga) from Beira Litoral, Portugal, showing spicy, solid fruit structure to mesh with the exotic textures and spices of the tagine. The Spanish Marqués de Riscal **Rioja Gran Reserva** (Tempranillo blend) distributes full-bodied fruit to highlight the subtle raisin flavors.

~ CHICKEN TAGINE ~
with Preserved Lemon & Green Olives

Tagine

6 cups chicken stock (page 159)

1 large carrot, peeled and cut into
¼-inch slices

1 turnip, halved vertically and cut into
¼-inch slices

1 small zucchini, cut into
¼-inch slices

½ cup unpitted green olives

3 slices preserved lemon (page 163)

1 chicken, cut into 8 pieces and skinned

2 tablespoons sliced almonds, toasted
(page 165)

3 dates

3 dried apricots

Pinch of ground cumin

Pinch of ground cinnamon

Pinch of cayenne pepper

Pinch of ground turmeric

About 3 saffron threads, or to taste

Salt & freshly ground pepper

Couscous

1 cup couscous

1 cup chicken stock (page 159), heated

3 tablespoons raisins

½ bunch mint, stemmed and cut into
fine julienne (about ¼ cup)

1 tablespoon sliced almonds, toasted
(page 165)

2 slices preserved lemon, finely chopped
(page 163)

8 black olives, pitted and cut into
small dice

½ tablespoon extra-virgin olive oil

Pinch of ground cumin

Salt & freshly ground pepper

Serves 4

CHEF'S NOTES Cook the tagine the day before and refrigerate it overnight for even more flavor. This classic Moroccan stew uses preserved lemons, which need to be prepared 1 month ahead of time, although you can buy them already prepared in specialty foods stores. The amount of saffron to use depends on the length of the threads and the intensity of their flavor. Adjust the amount accordingly.

PREPARATION To make the tagine: preheat the oven to 350°F. In a Dutch oven, combine the tagine ingredients, with salt and pepper to taste. Cover and bake for 45 minutes, or until the chicken is tender.

To make the couscous: spread the couscous in a sided baking sheet. Pour ½ cup of the stock over it and let sit for about 5 minutes. Roll the couscous between your palms to give the grain a polished look. Pour the remaining stock over it and let sit for 5 minutes. Add the raisins, mint, almonds, preserved lemon, olives, and olive oil. Season with the cumin, and salt and pepper to taste. Mix all the ingredients well.

TO SERVE Arrange a bed of couscous in the center of each plate. Top with the chicken tagine.

Perhaps more than any other recipe, this Hazelnut Pudding captures the luxury and sensual gratification of our desserts. The dense, yielding warmth of the pudding is gently cooled by the cream, with its classic Mediterranean infusion of fine Cognac. The light, crisp hazelnuts and the pudding's lush, dark, silken chocolate seem born for each other, producing a dessert of pure, intense pleasures.

Sometimes one wishes to change the way a dessert tastes on the palate between bites and other times one prefers to evoke its character, so we offer both options. We chose the Billecart-Salmon, **Rosé Champagne** from France to create lilting, fresh berry flavors on the palate with the rich texture of this pudding. To produce echoing flavors, we opted for the rarified Disznókö **Tokaji Aszú 6 Puttonyos** (Furmint/Hárslevelü), from the Tokaj-Hegyalja region of Hungary. Rich, sweet nut flavors abound from fork and glass alike as the senses work to keep abreast of this intriguing dessert.

∼ WARM CHOCOLATE-HAZELNUT PUDDING ∼
with Cognac Cream & Hot Chocolate Sauce

Chocolate-Hazelnut Pudding

Butter for greasing and sugar for dusting the darioles

4 tablespoons unsalted butter, at room temperature

2 tablespoons granulated sugar

3 eggs, separated

1 ounce semisweet chocolate, chopped

¾ cup hazelnuts, toasted (page 165), skinned (page 164), and ground

¼ cup finely ground ladyfingers

¼ cup all-purpose flour

Pinch of ground cinnamon

Pinch of ground cloves

Pinch of salt

A few drops of vanilla extract

Cognac Cream

1 cup heavy cream

¼ cup confectioners' sugar

1½ tablespoons Cognac or Brandy

Hot Chocolate Sauce (page 162)

Garnish

Fresh mint sprigs

Makes 6 individual puddings

CHEF'S NOTES The chocolate sauce may be replaced with a good-quality purchased chocolate sauce. You will need six 2¼-inch-diameter cone-shaped dariole dishes (available in some specialty cookware stores) to make this dessert, or six 3½-inch-diameter soufflé dishes may be substituted.

PREPARATION To make the pudding: grease the bottoms and sides of 6 cone-shaped dariole dishes (2¼ inches in diameter at the top, 1¾ inches at the bottom, and 2¼ inches tall) or six 3½-inch-diameter soufflé dishes with soft butter. Coat the bottoms and sides with sugar and tap out the excess. Place the dishes in the refrigerator.

Preheat the oven to 350°F. In a medium bowl, beat the butter and 1 tablespoon of the granulated sugar until light and fluffy. Beat in the egg yolks one at a time and continue to beat for 3 to 4 minutes, or until the batter is very smooth.

In a double boiler, melt the chocolate over barely simmering water. Carefully fold the chocolate into the butter mixture. Stir in the hazelnuts, ground ladyfingers, flour, spices, salt, and vanilla.

In a large bowl, beat the egg whites and remaining sugar until stiff, glossy peaks form. Stir one fourth of the egg whites into the chocolate mixture until blended. Gently fold in the remaining whites until blended.

Divide the chocolate mixture among the prepared dishes. Place the dishes in a baking pan and add hot water to come halfway up the sides of the dishes. Place the pan in the oven and bake the puddings for about 45 minutes, or until set.

To make the cream: in a deep bowl, beat the cream and sugar together until soft peaks form. Blend in the Cognac or Brandy and set aside.

Prepare the Hot Chocolate Sauce (page 162).

TO SERVE Run a knife around the edge of each pudding and invert to unmold in the center of each plate. Pour a large spoonful of chocolate sauce over one side of each pudding. Spoon the Cognac Cream on the other side. Garnish with a sprig of mint.

The soufflé symbolizes French culinary mastery, lending an air of drama and elegance that enhances even the most formal repast. Yet soufflés are surprisingly easy to make. The secret is in the beating of the eggs, the folding in of the ingredients, and your nose: a skilled chef never opens the oven to peek, waiting instead for the faint vanilla aroma that says the baking is complete.

The subtle orange flavors of this soufflé, framed by rich sweetness and airy textures, are delicious with a range of fine dessert wines and particularly good with a sweeter sparkling wine. Our cellar choice is Château Suduiraut **Sauternes** (Semillon/Sauvignon Blanc) from Bordeaux, France. Trumpeting honey and an apricot complexity, its resemblance to the Grand Marnier creates real synergy on the palate. A different sensation altogether also comes from France: Veuve-Clicquot's **Demi-Sec Champagne**, with a richness and beaded texture that elevates the flavors on the palate.

～ GRAND MARNIER SOUFFLÉ ～
with Negresco Sauce

Soufflé

Butter for greasing and sugar for dusting the soufflé dishes

1 cup milk

1 teaspoon vanilla extract

4 tablespoons unsalted butter, at room temperature

¾ cup all-purpose flour

6 eggs, separated

3 tablespoons Grand Marnier or other orange liqueur

Grated zest of 1 orange, blanched (page 158)

2 tablespoons cornstarch

¼ cup granulated sugar

Confectioners' sugar for dusting

Makes 6 individual soufflés

CHEF'S NOTES These soufflés can be refrigerated for up to 1 hour before being baked. Remove them from the refrigerator 15 minutes before baking.

PREPARATION Prepare the Negresco Sauce (page 163).

To make the soufflés: preheat the oven to 375°F. Grease the bottoms and sides of each of six 3½-inch soufflé dishes with softened butter. Dust the sides and bottoms of the dishes with granulated sugar and tap to remove the excess.

In a small saucepan, combine the milk and vanilla and bring to a boil. In a small bowl, mix the butter and the flour together. Whisk the butter mixture into the boiling milk mixture and cook, whisking constantly, for 4 minutes, or until slightly thickened. Remove from heat.

Beat the egg yolks into the mixture all at once. Beat in the liqueur and blanched zest until smooth. In a large bowl, mix the cornstarch and the granulated sugar together. Beat in the egg whites until stiff, glossy peaks form. Whisk one third of the méringue into the yolk mixture until blended. Fold in the remaining méringue until blended. Pour the mixture into the soufflé dishes and smooth the tops.

Place the dishes in a baking pan and add 1 inch of hot water to the pan. Bake for about 30 minutes, or until golden brown; do not open the oven during the first 15 minutes. Remove the soufflés from the oven.

TO SERVE Dust the soufflés with confectioners' sugar and serve immediately. Let each guest break open his or her soufflé with a spoon and pour in some of the Negresco Sauce.

When Europeans first tasted chocolate, they thought it had

magical powers. Our Chocolate Truffles prove them right.

The cocoa-coated crust melts away, revealing the soulful

sensuality of heavy cream, orange zest, Grand Marnier,

and dense, semi-sweet chocolate. If pleasure had a shape,

this would be it—still more proof that some of life's

deepest satisfactions happen during a great meal.

 Truffles are the ultimate after-dinner treat, yet few wines can stand up to their bitter, sweet strength. The Sandeman "Imperial" **20-year-old Tawny Port** from the Douro region of Portugal offers deep, heady flavors to carry the truffles perfectly. For a layering of contrasting flavors, the Kracher **Trockenbeerenauslese** "Grand Cuvée" (Zweigelt Rosé) from Neusiedlersee, Austria, shows an intensity of honey, dried apricots and mouth-watering acidity which shines through the density of the truffles. The alternating rich chocolate notes and exhilarating fruit flavors of this marriage are a wonderful way to end a meal.

～ CHOCOLATE TRUFFLES ～
with Orange & Grand Marnier Flavors

1 cup heavy cream

18 ounces semisweet chocolate, chopped, plus 2 ounces chopped separately

Grated zest of ½ orange, blanched (page 158)

Juice of ½ orange

1 cup Grand Marnier

⅓ cup unsalted butter

Unsweetened cocoa powder for coating

Makes 2½ dozen truffles

CHEF'S NOTES The truffle mixture can be prepared 1 day in advance and formed the day of serving.

PREPARATION In a medium saucepan, bring the cream to a boil. Add the 18 ounces chopped chocolate and stir until melted and smooth. Add the blanched zest, juice, Grand Marnier, and butter and stir until thoroughly mixed. Let cool. Cover and refrigerate for up to 24 hours.

Remove the truffle mixture from the refrigerator and let sit at room temperature for about 15 minutes. Meanwhile, in a double boiler, melt the reserved 2 ounces chopped chocolate over barely simmering water, stirring until smooth.

Form teaspoonfuls of the truffle mixture into one-inch-diameter balls. Using a wooden skewer, dip a truffle into the melted chocolate. Roll in the cocoa powder. Repeat to dip and coat the remaining truffles. Store in an airtight container in the refrigerator for up to 1 week.

TO SERVE Arrange truffles around a table filled with good friends, accompany with some leisure time to savor the culinary journey through the wide, delicious world of Crystal Cruises.

AIOLI

Makes ½ cup

½ cup mayonnaise

2 garlic cloves, minced

1 teaspoon Dijon mustard

1 tablespoon minced fresh curly parsley

Salt, cayenne pepper, & freshly ground white pepper

In a small bowl, combine all the ingredients, with salt and peppers to taste, and stir until blended.

ALFREDO SAUCE

Makes 3 cups

1 cup heavy cream

2 cups chicken stock (page 159)

3 tablespoons unsalted butter

¼ cup all-purpose flour

Salt & freshly ground white pepper

In a medium saucepan, bring the cream and chicken stock to a boil. Set aside and keep hot. In a medium, heavy saucepan, melt the butter over low heat. Stir in the flour and cook, stirring constantly, for 3 minutes. Remove the pan from heat and gradually whisk in the hot cream mixture. Add salt and pepper to taste.

Return to high heat and bring to a boil. Reduce heat and simmer for 20 minutes, stirring frequently. Pour through a fine-meshed sieve. Serve warm.

BASIL OIL

Makes ⅓ cup

¼ cup extra-virgin olive oil

Leaves from 6 fresh basil sprigs

Salt & freshly ground white pepper

In a blender or food processor, combine all the ingredients, with salt and pepper to taste, and

process until smooth. Strain through cheesecloth into a small bowl. Cover and refrigerate for up to 1 week.

BLANCHED CITRUS ZEST

Peel the colored zest from the fruit with a vegetable peeler, leaving the bitter white pith behind. Place the zest in a metal strainer in boiling water for 20 seconds and drain.

BOUQUET GARNI

1 fresh thyme sprig

1 bay leaf

3 fresh parsley sprigs

5 cracked black peppercorns

Tie ingredients together in a small piece of cheesecloth using kitchen string

BROWN VEAL STOCK

Makes 4 cups

2 pounds veal bones, cracked or cut into small pieces

½ tablespoon peanut oil

1 onion, quartered

1 carrot, peeled and quartered

1 celery stalk, chopped

1 tablespoon tomato paste

4 cups dry white wine

1 large tomato, chopped

½ unpeeled head garlic, halved crosswise

Bouquet garni: 1 fresh thyme sprig, 1 bay leaf, 3 fresh parsley sprigs, and 5 cracked black peppercorns tied together in a small piece of cheesecloth using kitchen string

Pinch of salt

Preheat the oven to 400°F. Put the bones and oil in a roasting pan and roast, stirring occasionally, until browned, about 15 minutes. Stir in the vegetables and the tomato paste and roast until the vegetables are lightly browned, about 5 minutes. (Take care not to let the vegetables brown too much, or the sauce will be bitter.)

Using a slotted spoon, transfer the bones and vegetables to a stockpot. Pour off the fat from the pan. Add the wine and cook over medium heat, stirring to scrape up the browned bits from the bottom of the pan. Add the tomato, garlic, bouquet garni, salt, and water to cover and bring to a boil over medium heat. Reduce heat to a simmer and skim the foam from the liquid. Partially cover and cook for about 45 minutes, skimming occasionally.

Strain the stock through a fine-meshed sieve, and refrigerate overnight. Remove and discard the congealed fat. Store the stock in the refrigerator for up to 3 days, or freeze for up to several weeks.

CANDIED LEMON ZEST

2 lemons

2 cups water

1 tablespoon sugar

Peel the colored zest from the lemons with a vegetable peeler, leaving the bitter white pith behind. Place the zest in a metal strainer in boiling water to cover for 20 seconds, drain, and rinse under cold water. Return the zest to the saucepan and add the 2 cups water and the sugar. Bring to a simmer and cook for about 25 minutes. Drain well and spread to cool.

CHEESE CROUTONS

Twelve ⅓-inch-thick slices baguette, toasted

1 garlic clove, halved lengthwise

Extra-virgin olive oil for brushing

¼ cup mixed shredded Parmesan and mozzarella cheese

Preheat the broiler. Rub each toasted crouton with a cut side of the garlic. Brush one side of each crouton with olive oil. Sprinkle the cheese mixture on top of the croutons. Place the croutons on a broiler pan lined with aluminum foil and broil until lightly browned, about 1 minute.

CHICKEN STOCK

Makes 8 cups

2 pounds chicken parts, such as backs and necks

3 quarts water

1 large onion, quartered

1 large carrot, peeled and quartered

1 celery stalk, chopped

Bouquet garni: 1 fresh thyme sprig, 1 bay leaf, 3 fresh parsley sprigs, and

5 cracked black peppercorns tied together in a small piece of cheesecloth using kitchen string

½ unpeeled head garlic, halved crosswise

1 large tomato, chopped

Rinse the chicken parts under very hot water. In a stockpot, combine the chicken parts and all the remaining ingredients. Bring to a boil over medium heat, skimming the foam frequently. Reduce heat to a simmer and cook for about 2 hours, skimming occasionally.

Strain the stock and taste. If the flavor is not concentrated, boil until reduced to your taste. Refrigerate the stock overnight. Remove and discard the congealed fat. Store the stock in the refrigerator for up to 3 days or freeze for up to several weeks.

CHOCOLATE COOKIES

Makes about 10 cookies

½ cup packed light brown sugar

⅓ cup unsalted butter, at room temperature

1 egg

3 ounces semisweet chocolate, chopped

1 ounce baking (unsweetened) chocolate, chopped

½ cup all-purpose flour

2 tablespoons unsweetened cocoa powder

½ teaspoon baking soda

Pinch of salt

Preheat the oven to 375°F. Line a baking sheet with parchment paper. In a medium bowl, beat the brown sugar and butter together until creamy. Beat in the egg until blended. Set aside.

In a double boiler, melt the two chocolates over barely simmering water. Pour into the butter mixture and stir until blended. Sift the flour, cocoa, baking soda, and salt into a medium bowl. Stir the flour mixture into the batter until thoroughly combined.

Drop heaping tablespoons of batter 1 inch apart on the prepared baking sheet. Bake for 25 minutes, or until firm. Transfer the cookies to wire racks to cool. Store in an airtight container for up to 1 week.

CHOCOLATE GÉNOISE CAKE

Chef's Note: This cake can be kept for several days in an airtight container, or it can be frozen.

Makes one 8-inch round cake, serves 6

4 eggs

½ cup sugar

¾ cup all-purpose flour

3 tablespoons unsweetened cocoa powder

Pinch of salt

4 tablespoons unsalted butter, melted

¼ teaspoon vanilla extract

Preheat the oven to 350°F. Brush an 8-inch round cake pan with melted butter. Using the bottom of the pan as a template, cut out a circle of waxed paper. Fit the paper into the pan and brush it with melted butter. Sprinkle the bottom and sides of the pan with flour and tap out the excess.

In a medium bowl, beat the eggs and sugar together until the mixture is pale in color and thick enough to leave a slowly dissolving ribbon trail on the surface of the batter when the whisk or beater is lifted. Sift the flour, cocoa, and salt together onto a square of waxed paper. Return the mixture to the sifter and sift about one third of it into the batter. Gently stir in the flour mixture with a wooden spoon. Repeat twice to sift and stir in all the flour mixture. Fold in the melted butter and vanilla until blended.

Pour the batter into the prepared pan and bake in the oven for 35 to 40 minutes, or until the cake has shrunk slightly from the sides of the pan and the top springs back when lightly pressed with a fingertip. Run a knife around the sides of the cake to loosen it, and invert the cake on a wire rack to cool completely.

CHOCOLATE TOPS

Chef's Note: The tops consist of 8 chocolate circles and 8 curled triangles. To make them, you will need three 8½-x-11-inch acetate sheets, a 3½-inch cookie cutter, and two 2½-inch-diameter cylinder forms.

6 ounces couverture bittersweet chocolate, chopped

Melt the chocolate in a double boiler over barely simmering water. Remove the double boiler from heat but leave the chocolate over the hot water. Place two 8½-inch acetate sheets on a flat work surface. Pour ½ cup melted chocolate over the acetate sheets and spread with a spatula to a thickness of about 1/16 inch. Let cool until the chocolate is firm. Using a 3½-inch cookie cutter, cut out 4 circles from each sheet. Return the leftover chocolate to the double boiler and mix thoroughly to melt.

Cut 2 triangular templates from the remaining 8½-x-11-inch acetate sheet to these dimensions: 8½ inches wide at the base, 5 inches on one side, and 10 inches on the third side. Lay the templates on a work surface, preferably a marble slab. Pour 3 tablespoons of the melted chocolate onto a template and spread with a spatula to cover the template. Lift the template. Return any of the overflow to the double boiler.

Before the chocolate sets, bend the 8½-inch side of the triangle into a tubular form with the chocolate on the inside (see photograph, page 96). Slide into a 2½-inch-diameter cylinder form. Repeat with the second template. Refrigerate. When the triangles have set, about 10 minutes, remove each from the form and peel off the acetate. Repeat to make a total of 8 curled triangles.

CLARIFIED BUTTER

Melt the butter over low heat. Spoon off the froth at the top

and carefully pour the melted butter into a clean jar, leaving behind the milky sediment at the bottom. Store in the refrigerator indefinitely.

CRÈME ANGLAISE
Makes 2¼ cups
2 cups milk
6 egg yolks
¼ cup sugar
¼ teaspoon vanilla extract

In a medium saucepan, heat the milk over medium heat until bubbles form around the edges of the pan. In a medium bowl, whisk the egg yolks and sugar together. Gradually whisk the hot milk into the egg yolks.

Return the mixture to the pan and cook over medium heat, stirring constantly with a wooden spatula, until slightly thickened (the custard will coat the spatula). Do not overcook or boil the custard or it will curdle. Stir in the vanilla extract.

Strain the custard through a fine-meshed sieve into a medium bowl. Set the bowl in a larger bowl filled with ice cubes and let cool, or cover and refrigerate until cold, about 2 hours. May be refrigerated for up to 3 days.

• COFFEE CRÈME ANGLAISE
Prepare the Crème Anglaise recipe above using only 1 cup milk. After whisking the yolks and sugar together, whisk in *1 cup cold brewed espresso* until very well blended.

• COGNAC CRÈME ANGLAISE
Prepare the Crème Anglaise recipe above, adding *1 tablespoon Cognac or Brandy* with the vanilla extract.

DEMI-GLACE

Makes about ¾ cup

In a medium, heavy saucepan, boil 4 cups brown veal stock (page 158) until reduced to about ¾ cup. As it reduces, change to smaller saucepans and lower the heat to avoid scorching. Store in an airtight container in the refrigerator for up to 3 days, or freeze for up to several weeks.

DUCK STOCK

Makes 3 cups

2 duck carcasses, including neck bones

1 tablespoon duck fat or canola oil

1 large onion, chopped

1 large carrot, peeled and chopped

1 leek, white part only, washed and chopped

1 celery stalk, chopped

2 unpeeled garlic cloves

2 large tomatoes, chopped

1 tablespoon tomato paste

4 cups brown veal stock (page 158)

3 cups water

Chop each carcass into 5 pieces. In a stockpot, melt the duck fat or heat the oil over medium heat. Add the carcass pieces and necks and cook, stirring occasionally, for about 5 minutes, or until browned. Add the onion, carrot, leek, celery, and garlic and cook, stirring occasionally, for about 4 minutes. Pour off all

the fat. Stir in the tomatoes and tomato paste and cook for about 2 minutes. Add the veal stock and water, bring to a boil, reduce heat, and simmer, partially covered, for about 2 hours, skimming the fat from the top of the liquid frequently, Strain through a fine-meshed sieve into a saucepan. Cover and store in the refrigerator for up to 3 days, or freeze for up to 3 months.

FISH STOCK

Chef's Note: Fish skin should not be included in the stock, as it will cause the liquid to darken.

Makes 6 cups

½ cup chopped mushrooms or mushroom stems

1 large onion, sliced

1 celery stalk, chopped

1 leek, white part only, chopped

1½ pounds fish bones, broken into pieces and very well washed (if fish heads are included, remove gills first)

6 cups water

Bouquet garni: 1 fresh thyme sprig, 1 bay leaf, 3 fresh parsley sprigs, and 5 cracked black peppercorns tied together in a small piece of cheesecloth using kitchen string

1½ cups dry white wine

In a stockpot, combine all the ingredients and bring to a boil. Reduce heat and simmer for 35 minutes, skimming occasionally. Strain through a fine-meshed sieve. Let cool, cover, and refrigerate for up to 3 days, or freeze for up to several weeks.

HAZELNUT MÉRINGUE

Makes one 9-by-12-inch méringue

2 egg whites

¼ cup confectioners' sugar

3 tablespoons granulated sugar

½ cup hazelnuts, toasted, skinned, and finely ground (page 164)

2 teaspoons flour

Preheat the oven to 400°F. Line a baking sheet with parchment paper.

In a large bowl, combine the egg whites, confectioners' sugar, and granulated sugar and beat until soft peaks form. In a small bowl, mix the hazelnuts and flour together. Gradually fold the hazelnut mixture into the méringue mixture. Mound the méringue mixture on the prepared baking sheet. With a spatula, spread the mixture evenly into a 12-inch square. Bake the méringue for 10 to 15 minutes, or until a light golden brown. Remove the pan from the oven.

HONEYED PECAN HALVES

Makes garnish for 4 servings or more

1 pound shelled pecan halves

1½ cups sugar

1½ cups water

2 tablespoons corn oil

Soak pecan halves in water to cover for about 15 minutes, then drain well. Fill a large pot with water and bring to a boil. Add the nuts and cook for about 10 minutes. Drain, rinse under cool water, and drain again.

Bring the sugar and the 1½ cups water to a boil in medium pot over medium heat for about 2 minutes or until the sugar is dissolved. Add the nuts, reduce the heat to low, and stir well with a wooden spoon. Simmer the nuts for about 15 minutes in the syrup, stirring often, until they are well coated with the syrup. Add some water if the syrup becomes too sticky. Remove from the heat and let the nuts cool in the syrup for another 10 minutes.

Preheat the oven to 350°F.

Strain the excess syrup, toss the nuts with the oil, and spread them on a large nonstick baking sheet. Bake for about 30 minutes, stirring occasionally, until they are crisp and dry. Store in a tightly closed container at room temperature.

HOT CHOCOLATE SAUCE
Makes 2 cups

½ cup heavy cream or half-and-half

8 ounces semisweet chocolate, chopped

4 tablespoons unsalted butter

In a small saucepan, heat the cream or half-and-half until bubbles form around the edges. Put the chocolate in a double boiler over barely simmering water. Pour the hot cream or half-and-half over the chocolate. Add the butter and whisk all the ingredients together until melted and smooth.

LOBSTER STOCK
Makes 2 cups

2 tablespoons extra-virgin olive oil

2 lobster shells, crushed

3 shallots, sliced

1 carrot, peeled and chopped

½ celery stalk, chopped

1 small leek, white part only, sliced

1 tablespoon tomato paste

1 bay leaf

2 fresh thyme sprigs

2 fresh tarragon sprigs

1 tablespoon Cognac or Brandy

1 cup dry white wine

1 pound tomatoes, peeled, seeded, and chopped (page 163)

3 cups water

Freshly ground white pepper

In a large, heavy saucepan over high heat, heat the olive oil and sauté the lobster shells for 2 to 3 minutes, or until brilliant red. Reduce heat to medium and add the shallots, carrot, celery, and leek and sauté for about 4 minutes, or until the leek and shallots are translucent. Stir in the tomato paste. Cook for 1 minute.

Add the bay leaf, thyme, tarragon, and Cognac or Brandy. Heat for several seconds, then light the mixture with a long-handled match. Shake the pan until the flames subside. Add the wine and cook for about 5 minutes, or until the mixture is reduced by two thirds. Reduce heat, add the tomatoes and water, and simmer, uncovered, for 25 minutes. Add the pepper to taste. Strain through a fine-meshed sieve. Let cool, cover, and refrigerate for up to 3 days or freeze for up to several weeks.

MASHED POTATOES
Serves 6

3 large russet potatoes

Salt

½ cup heavy cream

4 tablespoons unsalted butter

¼ cup milk

In a large pot of salted boiling water, cook the potatoes until tender, about 20 minutes; the blade of a paring knife should pass easily through the center of each potato. Drain.

Holding the hot potatoes in a towel, peel off the skins. Meanwhile, bring the cream, butter, and milk to a boil, seasoning with salt to taste; set aside and keep warm. Cut the potatoes into chunks and pass them through a potato ricer into a warm bowl. Or, mash them in the pot they were cooked in, using a potato masher. Add the hot cream mixture and stir until blended.

MASHED SWEET POTATOES
Serves 4

12 ounces sweet potatoes, baked, peeled, and mashed

¼ cup milk, heated

2 tablespoons heavy cream

Salt & freshly ground pepper

Pinch of ground cumin

In a blender or food processor, combine the sweet potatoes, ¼ cup milk, and cream. Add salt and pepper to taste and the cumin and blend until smooth. Transfer the mashed sweet potatoes to a small pan and heat through over low heat, stirring frequently. If needed for the proper consistency, add a little more milk.

MAYONNAISE

Makes 1 cup

1 egg yolk

2 tablespoons tarragon or white wine vinegar

1 teaspoon Dijon mustard

Salt & freshly ground white pepper

1 cup olive or canola oil

With a whisk, beat together the egg yolk, vinegar, mustard, and salt and pepper to taste. While whisking constantly, pour the oil in a few drops at a time, then in a very thin stream until the mayonnaise has emulsified. Or, combine all the ingredients except the oil in a blender or food processor. With the machine running, gradually add the oil in a very thin stream until the mixture has emulsified. Store in an airtight container in the refrigerator for up to 3 days.

NEGRESCO SAUCE

Makes about 2¼ cups

2 cups milk

6 egg yolks

¼ cup sugar

2 tablespoons Grand Marnier or other orange-flavored liqueur

Grated zest of 1 orange

¼ teaspoon vanilla extract

Prepare the Crème Anglaise recipe on page 160, adding 2 tablespoons Grand Marnier and grated zest of 1 orange with the vanilla extract.

ORANGE GARNISH

2 oranges

2 cups water

Pinch of sugar

Peel the orange-colored zest from the oranges with a vegetable peeler, leaving the bitter white pith behind. Cut the zest into fine julienne.

Using a large knife, cut off the top and bottom of each orange down to the flesh. Put each orange on end and cut off the pith down to the flesh. Cut out each orange segment from between the membrane and place in a bowl. Squeeze the juice from the membranes over the orange segments and set the segments aside.

Put the orange zest in a small saucepan, add water to cover, bring to boil, and cook for about 1 minute. Drain the zest and rinse under cold water. Return the zest to the saucepan and add the 2 cups water and sugar. Bring to a simmer and cook for about 25 minutes. Drain and allow to cool.

PEELING AND SEEDING TOMATOES

Cut an X in the bottom of each tomato. Plunge the tomatoes into a large pan of boiling water and blanch for 1 minute. Using a slotted spoon, transfer the tomatoes to a bowl of ice water to cool slightly. Using a small knife, peel the skin from the tomatoes. To seed the tomatoes, cut them in half and hold them upside down over a sink (or a bowl, to reserve the juice), squeezing them gently and shaking them to release the seeds.

PRESERVED LEMONS

Makes about ½ cup

6 lemons, scrubbed and cut into ½-inch-thick crosswise slices

Juice of 4 lemons, or as needed to cover the lemon slices

1 tablespoon salt

Pinch each of ground cumin, ground cinnamon, and ground nutmeg

In a small glass or ceramic bowl, combine all the ingredients. Cover tightly with plastic wrap or a lid and refrigerate for 30 days.

RASPBERRY COULIS

Makes 2 cups

2 cups fresh raspberries, fresh or thawed unsweetened frozen

1 to 2 tablespoons confectioners' sugar

In a blender or food processor, purée the raspberries until smooth. Add the sugar and purée again. Strain through a fine-meshed sieve into a bowl. Cover and refrigerate for at least 1 hour, or up to 3 days.

SAUTÉED SPINACH

Serves 4

1½ tablespoons extra-virgin olive oil

4 cups packed fresh spinach leaves

Salt & freshly ground pepper

In a large sauté pan or skillet over high heat, heat the olive oil and sauté the spinach leaves for about 1 minute, or until wilted. Add the salt and pepper to taste.

SAUTÉED SPINACH WITH CHANTERELLES

Serves 4

Chef's Note: **Other types of fresh mushrooms may be used in place of the chanterelles.**

1 tablespoon extra-virgin olive oil

6 ounces chanterelle mushrooms, finely sliced

1 garlic clove, thinly sliced

1 tablespoon finely sliced green onion, white part only

2 bunches water spinach (available in Asian markets) or regular spinach, stemmed, well washed, and blanched

Salt & freshly ground white pepper

In a large sauté pan or skillet over high heat, heat the olive oil and sauté the chanterelles for about 2 minutes, or until lightly golden. Add the garlic, green onion, and spinach and sauté for about 2 minutes. Season with salt and pepper to taste.

SLOW-ROASTED TOMATOES

Serves 2 as a garnish

2 tablespoons extra-virgin olive oil

2 Roma (plum) tomatoes, each cut into 6 wedges

1 garlic clove, halved

1 shallot, halved

2 fresh thyme sprigs

2 small bay leaves

6 large fresh basil leaves

Pinch of sugar

Salt & freshly ground white pepper

Preheat the oven to 300°F. In a medium baking pan, combine all the ingredients, with salt and pepper to taste. Cover with aluminum foil and bake for 10 minutes. Remove the foil and bake 5 minutes longer, or until the tomatoes are soft but not falling apart. Serve warm.

SKINNING HAZELNUTS

Wrap hot toasted hazelnuts in a kitchen towel and let sit a few minutes, then rub them together inside the towel to remove as many skins as possible.

STEWED LENTILS

Makes 3 cups

1½ cups dried brown lentils, picked over, rinsed, and soaked for 30 minutes in cold water and drained

1 carrot, peeled and halved lengthwise

1 onion, halved crosswise

1 celery stalk, halved lengthwise

Bouquet garni: 1 fresh thyme sprig, 1 bay leaf, 3 fresh parsley sprigs, and 5 cracked black peppercorns tied together in a small piece of cheesecloth using kitchen string

In a soup pot, combine all the ingredients and bring to a boil.

Reduce heat, cover, and simmer for 30 minutes, or until the lentils are tender but not mushy. Remove and discard the bouquet garni.

STRAWBERRY COULIS

Makes 2 cups

2 cups fresh strawberries, hulled

1 to 2 tablespoons confectioners' sugar

In a blender or food processor, purée the strawberries until smooth. Add the sugar and purée again. Strain through a fine-meshed sieve into a bowl. Cover and refrigerate for at least 1 hour, or up to 3 days.

SUN-DRIED TOMATO CONFIT

Serves 4

½ tablespoon extra-virgin olive oil

1 shallot, finely diced

¼ cup oil-packed sun-dried tomatoes, drained and julienned

¼ cup dry red wine

2 large fresh basil leaves, julienned

Salt & freshly ground white pepper

In a small sauté pan or skillet over medium heat, heat the olive oil and sauté the shallot for about 2 minutes, or until translucent. Reduce heat to low. Add the tomatoes and wine and cook for about 4 minutes, or until the wine is reduced by about two thirds. Add the basil and salt and pepper to taste.

SWEET PASTRY CRUST

Makes one 9- or 10-inch tart shell or 8 tartlet shells

1¾ cups all-purpose flour

Pinch of salt

⅓ cup sugar

4 egg yolks

⅛ teaspoon vanilla extract

½ cup (1 stick) cold unsalted butter, cut into small pieces

In a medium bowl, stir the flour, salt, and sugar together. Stir in the egg yolks and vanilla extract until blended. Add the butter and work it into the flour mixture with your fingers until the mixture resembles coarse crumbs. Using a dough scraper or spatula, mix the dough with a cutting motion until smooth.

Turn the dough out on a lightly floured board and, using the heel of one hand, push it away in small portions until all the dough has been smeared. Gather the dough up with a dough scraper or spatula and press the dough into a ball. Wrap in plastic wrap and refrigerate for at least 30 minutes or up to 3 days.

To prebake the crust: preheat the oven to 375°F. On a lightly floured board, roll the dough out to a 13-inch circle. Fit the dough into a 9- or 10-inch tart pan and run the rolling pin across the top of the pan to trim off the dough. Pierce the bottom of the crust all over with a fork. Fit a piece of parchment paper into the crust and fill with dried beans or pie weights. Bake the crust for 15 to 20 minutes, or until lightly browned. Let cool on a wire rack.

To make eight 3-inch tartlet shells: roll the dough out to a 13-inch circle. Using a 5-inch round cookie cutter, cut out 8 rounds. Fit each into a 3-inch tartlet mold. Pierce the bottom of the crust all over with a fork. Fit a piece of parchment paper into each crust and fill with dried beans or pie weights. Bake the crusts for 15 minutes, or until lightly browned. Let cool on a wire rack.

SWEET TEMPURA BATTER

Makes approximately 2 cups

1 tablespoon cornstarch, plus more for dusting

¼ cup rice flour

1 tablespoon baking soda

1 tablespoon confectioners' sugar

¼ cup granulated sugar

Pinch of salt

Pinch each of ground cinnamon, ground nutmeg, and ground cumin

Juice of ½ lemon

⅛ teaspoon vanilla extract

½ cup ice water

In a small bowl, mix all the dry ingredients together. Add the lemon juice and vanilla, and gradually whisk in the ice water. Dust more cornstarch over whatever is to be battered.

TOASTING SEEDS AND NUTS

Preheat the oven to 350°F. Spread the seeds or nuts on a sided baking sheet and toast in the oven, stirring once or twice, until lightly golden, about 5 minutes for seeds and 8 minutes for nuts.

TOMATO-BASIL SAUCE

Makes 4 cups

2 tablespoons olive oil

2 shallots, minced

1 garlic clove, minced

2 pounds tomatoes, peeled, seeded, and chopped (page 163)

1 tablespoon tomato paste

¼ cup dry red wine

Salt & freshly ground white pepper

1 bay leaf

2 basil sprigs, plus 4 large basil leaves, chopped

1 cup water

In a medium saucepan over medium heat, heat the olive oil and sauté the shallots for about 3 minutes, or until translucent. Add the garlic and sauté for 1 minute. Add the tomatoes, tomato paste, wine, and salt and pepper to taste. Cook until reduced by half. Add the bay leaf, basil sprigs, and water. Cover and simmer for about 45 minutes, stirring occasionally. Add the chopped basil. Taste and adjust the seasoning. Serve warm.

VANILLA ICE CREAM

Makes 1 quart

2 cups milk or half-and-half

1 cup heavy cream

2 vanilla beans, halved lengthwise, or 1 teaspoon vanilla extract

5 egg yolks

½ cup sugar

In a medium saucepan, combine the milk or half-and-half and cream. Scrape the pulp from the vanilla beans, if using, and add the pulp and the beans to the pan. Heat the mixture over medium heat until bubbles form around the edges of the pan. In a medium bowl, whisk the egg yolks and sugar together. Gradually whisk the hot milk mixture into the yolk mixture.

Return the mixture to the pan and cook over medium heat, stirring constantly with a wooden spatula, until slightly thickened (the custard will coat the spatula). Do not overcook or boil the custard or it will curdle. Stir in the vanilla extract now, if using.

Strain the custard through a fine-meshed sieve into a medium bowl. Set the bowl in a larger bowl filled with ice cubes to cool, or cover and place in the refrigerator until cold. Freeze the cold custard in an ice cream maker according to the manufacturer's instructions.

VEGETABLE STOCK

Makes 8 cups

8 ounces cauliflower, chopped

8 ounces zucchini, chopped

1 leek, white part only, chopped

1 large onion, chopped

1 large carrot, peeled and chopped

1 celery stalk, chopped

8 ounces mushrooms, chopped

Bouquet garni: 1 fresh thyme sprig, 1 bay leaf, 3 fresh parsley sprigs, and 5 cracked black peppercorns tied together in a small piece of cheesecloth using kitchen string

½ unpeeled head garlic, halved crosswise

1 large tomato, chopped

2 quarts water

In a stockpot, combine all the ingredients. Bring to a boil over medium heat. Reduce heat to a simmer and cook for about 1 hour, skimming occasionally.

Strain the stock and taste. If the flavor is not concentrated, boil until reduced to your taste. Refrigerate the stock overnight. Store in the refrigerator for up to 3 days or freeze for up to several weeks.

WAFFLE POTATOES

Makes garnish for 4 portions

3 cups vegetable oil for deep-frying

1 large russet potato, peeled and cut into 1/16-inch-thick slices on a mandoline with a waffle blade

Salt

In a Dutch oven or deep fryer, heat the oil to 375°F. Never fill the pan more than one-third full, in order to prevent splashing or overflowing of the fat. Use a deep-fat thermometer and

follow the cooking temperature specified. Add the potato slices and deep-fry for 1 minute, or until golden brown. Using a slotted spoon or a wire-mesh skimmer, transfer to paper towels to drain. Sprinkle with salt to taste. Keep warm in a low oven until serving.

WHITE CHOCOLATE LATTICE

2 ounces white chocolate coating, chopped

Cut eight 2½-by-8-inch strips of acetate. In a double boiler, melt the coating over barely simmering water. Fit a pastry bag with a very thin writing tip and fill it with the melted coating. Pipe a diagonal lattice pattern over one of the acetate strips (see photograph, page 98). Before the coating sets, wrap the acetate around a cake, with the chocolate side in. Repeat until all the cakes are wrapped. Refrigerate for 15 minutes. Remove acetate before serving.

~ INDEX ~

METRIC CONVERSIONS

Liquid Weights

U.S. Measurement	Metric Equivalent
¼ teaspoon	1.23 ml
½ teaspoon	2.5 ml
¾ teaspoon	3.7 ml
1 teaspoon	5 ml
1 tablespoon (3 teaspoons)	15 ml
2 tablespoons (1 ounce)	15 ml
¼ cup	60 ml
⅓ cup	80 ml
½ cup	120 ml
⅔ cup	160 ml
¾ cup	180 ml
1 cup (8 ounces)	240 ml
2 cups (1 pint)	480 ml
3 cups	720 ml
4 cups (1 quart)	1 litre
4 quarts (1 gallon)	3¾ litres

Dry Weights

U.S. Measurement	Metric Equivalent
¼ ounce	7 grams
⅓ ounce	10 grams
½ ounce	14 grams
1 ounce	28 grams
1½ ounces	42 grams
1¾ ounces	50 grams
2 ounces	57 grams
3 ounces	85 grams
3½ ounces	100 grams
4 ounces (¼ pound)	114 grams
6 ounces	170 grams
8 ounces (½ pound)	227 grams
9 ounces	250 grams
16 ounces (1 pound)	464 grams
1.1 pounds	500 grams
2.2 pounds	1,000 grams

Temperatures

Fahrenheit	Celsius (Centigrade)
32°F (water freezes)	0° C
200°F	95° C
212°F (water boils)	100° C
225°F	110° C
250°F	120° C
275°F	135° C
300°F (low oven)	150° C
325°F	160° C
350°F (moderate oven)	175° C
375°F	190° C
400°F (hot oven)	205° C
425°F	220° C
450°F (very hot oven)	230° C
475°F	245° C
500°F (extremely hot oven)	360° C

~ ACKNOWLEDGEMENTS ~

EXECUTIVE STAFF

President, Joseph Watters
Senior Vice President Hotel
    Operations, Dietmar Wertanzl
Senior Vice President Finance,
    Gregg Michel
Vice President Marketing,
    Adam Leavitt
Vice President Purchasing,
    Robert Koven

CREATIVE TEAM

Culinary Director, Toni Neumeister
Designer/Producer, Elizabeth Hecker
Photographer, Deborah Jones
Photographer's Assistant, Jeri Jones
Photography Stylist, Sara Slavin
Food Stylist, Amy Nathan

Additional photo credits:
Danny Lehman - cover ship, ship on
curved horizon, page 100; Glenn
Cormier - end papers, pages 15 and
70; Michael Venera - woman at stern;
Robert Whitman - guests dining;
Gabor Geissler/Tony Stone Images -
page 4; Harvey Lloyd - page 16; Steven
Rothfeld/Tony Stone Images - page
17; Roger Paperno - pages 44, 126 and
172; Penny Tweedie/Tony Stone
Images - page 45; Gary Hubbell/
Tony Stone Images - page 71; David
Austen/FPG International - page 101;
Michael Busselle/Tony Stone Images -
page 127; Jan Butchofsky - aft wake.

SUPPLIERS

We would like to thank all our suppliers
who define our quality standards and
never let us down, especially those who
assisted with our photo shoot.

Special appreciation goes to our table-
top suppliers who provided a variety of
pieces from their collections to add
diversity to our photographs: Villeroy &
Boch (china, glassware, and flatware),
Wedgwood (china), Bernardaud (china),
Reidel (crystal), Elkington Silversmiths
(flatware), and Frette Linens.

We would like to thank the following
food suppliers for providing the special
items we needed for the recipes:
City Seafood, Colorado Boxed Beef,
American Fish & Seafood Co.,
Northern Produce, Wing Kee Produce,
and West Coast Ship Chandlers.

This project was a great dream, which required the efforts of countless people to become a reality. First of all, a special thank you to Joseph Watters, Dietmar Wertanzl, and Gregg Michel for their vision and confidence in this project. Thank you to Toni Neumeister and his team at sea and ashore for bringing our culinary standards to such great heights and to Elizabeth Hecker for her creative spirit and tireless energy, which gave shape to every part of this project.

Few photographers could capture the spirit of life at sea and the essence of each recipe as beautifully as Deborah Jones. Thank you to Deborah for her commitment to excellence and to her assistant Jeri Jones, who brought harmony to each set. Special thanks go also to Sara Slavin, whose friendship and talent supported this book from beginning to end; and to Amy Nathan, whose expertise and finely tuned intuition perfected each recipe presentation for the camera.

Thank you to Francis Manzett for making all our culinary thoughts become reality in words. To Cathleen Vickers, the ultimate teammate, thank you for your diligence and good humor. Much appreciation goes to George Rice & Sons, and their color department, who took care of our more unique separations. And very special thanks to Jacques Pépin, Wolfgang Puck, Barbara Tropp, and Charles Dale, for donating their recipes as a souvenir of our cooking together on board, and especially André Soltner, not only for his recipe but also for the very kind words for our Preface. And thanks to Kirk Frederick, for his wholehearted support.

Including wine pairings for our recipes was an important and natural thing to do, requiring the talents and hard work of many people both on board and ashore. Our sincerest gratitude goes to Bob Roux for his love of the noble grape that helped shape and form our pairings; to the palate of our Culinary Director, who never forgets a taste; to our Cellarmasters, Jan Sørrenson, Dietmar Duller, and Bernhard Wernig and their fine staff of sommeliers for their expertise; to Laely Heron for her masterful advice; to Gilian Handleman for her eloquent prose; and to Scott Torrance for his vast knowledge and enthusiastic support.

Thank you to Patrick Martin, Master Chef, Le Cordon Bleu, for his dedicated friendship and technical expertise, and recipe editor Carolyn Miller for her attention to detail. Thanks to our Executive Pastry Chefs for helping to craft our dessert recipes to perfection: Hans Kiendle, Harry Neufang, and Joachim Holter. And, to Chefs de Cuisine Kunioki Wakasugi (Kyoto) and John Juan Po (Jade Garden) for lending their culinary expertise to our Asian-inspired recipes. To the Chefs de Cuisine, Prego, Rolf Weber, Kim Birk, and Bruno Reichart, and especially Renate Fürnhammer, thank you for assisting with all the food preparation for the photography. As well, many thanks to the Chefs de Cuisine in the main galleys, Harry Gramm and Gerhard Egger, and their fine team of professionals who supported the shoot while attending to their normal list of responsibilities. And a very special thanks to Executive Chefs Juergen Klocker, Fritz Pilz, Guenter Lorenz, and Markus Nufer, who maintain our high quality standards on a daily basis.

Provisioning for the photography in this book required the talents of a first-class team: many thanks to Allen Nino for his continual search of world markets for the finest food and wine products, and to Brian Kimura for making sure it is always delivered wherever in the world the ships happen to be. Thanks also to our ships' stores managers Anders Björkman, Richard Paulsen, Mikael Finnas, and Michael Kowatsch for keeping it all organized once it arrives on board.

Special thanks to the Maîtres d'Hôtel, Josef Widmar, Jacques Martin, Phillip Smith, Leo Assmair, Mario Pires, Antonio Santomera, and their team of dedicated headwaiters and waiters, and the bar staff who endured our daily disruptions to their schedules; to the Food & Beverage Managers, Hubert Buelacher, Josef Lumetsberger, and Jacques Wulffaert, who supported us totally from beginning to end; and our Hotel Directors Josef Matt, Per Nilsen, Herbert Jaeger, Herbert Doppler, and Thomas Mazloum, you have a gift for hospitality.

To Captains Reidulf Maalen, Helge Brudvik, Glenn Edvardsen, John Økland, and the Bridge, thank you for your enthusiasm for this project and understanding when we needed the perfect light, and to the Deck Department and Housekeeping, who keep the ships sparkling, making each background inspiring.

Without the enthusiasm of our guests and all the staff of Crystal Cruises, this book would never have come into being. All of you are Crystal Family. Thank you, this book is for you!

Library of Congress Cataloging-in-Publication Data

Crystal Cruises
The Crystal Cruises Cookbook: Recipes inspired by the world in which we sail…
Includes index.
ISBN 0-9675032-0-5

1. Cookery.   2. Cookery International.   3. Cruising.
I. Crystal Cruises   II. Title.

Library of Congress Card Number: 99-067100

Printed in Japan, by Toppan Printing
First Printing 1999

Distributed by Crystal Cruises
2049 Century Park East, Suite 1400
Los Angeles, California 90067
310.785.9300
www.crystalcruises.com

CRYSTAL CRUISES